ARGUING WITH GOD

ARGUING WITH GOD

A DIALOGUE: FUNDAMENTALIST CHRISTIANITY VERSUS THE GAYS

J. T. HUTCHERSON

iUniverse, Inc.
Bloomington

Arguing with God
A Dialogue: Fundamentalist Christianity versus the Gays

Front cover concept by J. T. Hutcherson

iUniverse books may be ordered through booksellers or by contacting:

iUniverse
1663 Liberty Drive
Bloomington, IN 47403
www.iuniverse.com
1-800-Authors (1-800-288-4677)

Because of the dynamic nature of the Internet, any web addresses or links contained in this book may have changed since publication and may no longer be valid. The views expressed in this work are solely those of the author and do not necessarily reflect the views of the publisher, and the publisher hereby disclaims any responsibility for them.

Any people depicted in stock imagery provided by Thinkstock are models, and such images are being used for illustrative purposes only.

Certain stock imagery © Thinkstock.

ISBN: 978-1-4502-9554-3 (sc)
ISBN: 978-1-4502-9555-0 (ebk)

Printed in the United States of America

iUniverse rev. date: 02/15/2011

For Mary and Jamison

CONTENTS

AUTHOR'S NOTE

"He hath shewed thee, oh man, what is good; and what doth the Lord require of thee but to do justly, and to love mercy, and to walk humbly with thy God?" —Micah 6:8 (KJV)

Attempts to follow the guidance of Micah often fail. What is the just action? What is the merciful response to our brother? Does looking beneath the surface of our belief mean we are not walking humbly with God? Is humility blind obedience? Is the Bible a technical instruction book—merely a how-to manual? Does it communicate only literally, or are we responsible for determining justice, mercy, and humility continually?

When I was a very young man attending an extremely fundamentalist, wonderfully Pentecostal-style, nondenominational church, all these questions found ready answers in the Authorized King James Version of the Holy Bible. Thou shalt do this, and thou shalt not do this—the answers were spelled out in holy, onion-skinned, Elizabethan English.

Justice, at that time, equated obedience. The Bible said it, and that was good enough. Education appeared to be superfluous. Literary devices, poetic interpretation, and historical context existed only in the worldly, academic realm. One did not need these to understand the Bible. Mercy seemed just as easy to assess. Compassion and forgiveness characterized God; that was mercy. Likewise, practicing humility would be admitting God was in charge, and man was subservient; bow down before him. Again, following Micah's counsel entailed only obedience.

My conflict between obedience and justice began to develop during the years I was studying for my degrees at the university. Since it was the Vietnam War era, most questions of obedience concerned government more than God. Nevertheless, I discovered then that one is obligated to determine the justice within one's obedience. Justice involved finding the right and then obeying one's conscience or obeying the law—whichever was the right. Even our government recognized this potential conflict, as exceptions to the military draft existed for "reasons of conscience." The challenging question, then, was deeper: what does obedience require? Today, the threats, accusations, and curses exchanged between the various camps—the Christians, the gays, and the allies of each—rest on obedience. It is obedience to "what" that divides them.

Do we obey a literal interpretation of an inerrant Bible, or do we have a responsibility to understand the various books of the Bible within their own time and cultural milieu? Perhaps we ought to consider the human perspective of the authors and recognize the paradigms from which they wrote. Even further, we can easily see God as one who knows more of science, astronomy, physics, cosmology, psychology, and physiology than the early writers and prophets. Is it not probable that he would still have allowed, even expected, the earliest biblical authors to write from their personal perspective of truth—even when they were in error scientifically? Would he really have felt the need to correct Joshua or any other writer and explain to him the actual form of the solar system or the vastness of the universe?

We, too, must obey the fullest and most thoughtful meanings of justice, mercy, and humility discoverable within our own time and place. Obedience, then, becomes a broader and richer assignment than simply observing most ancient laws or even the Ten Commandments. God asks us all to seek and to find the truths demanded in the graceful words, "to do justly, and to love mercy, and to walk humbly with our God."

If we look through the eyes of justice, we can see more clearly. It is nearly impossible for an educated, aware, thinking, or caring person to perceive homosexuality as a personal choice that one makes. If that were true, all the so-called straight people would really be walking around lusting after their own gender but hiding it, having "chosen" to hook up heterosexually.

It is also nearly impossible for any person to deny that several of the biblical writers appear to condemn homosexuality—or in Paul's case, identify it as a punishment one receives for denying or defying God.[i] Now, how do we as caring and even faithful human beings accept these two impossibilities and maintain the concept of a just and caring deity?

The Episcopal Church, for example, has long understood that God is revealed through personal experience, that there is a balance between biblical teaching and thought, and that history is a map of where we have been—not a parking lot for the future. Presumably, most all the Christian churches in the world know how to find the answer to the homosexual questions.

The fundamentalists, conservatives, evangelicals, liberals, and even moderns only have to answer the abused and misused question, "What would Jesus do?" Regardless of whether one sees the Christ as a symbol or metaphor, living or dead, real or a creation beyond his own purposes, would he have said to the woman brought to him by her accusers that he totally understood her predicament, but that it would be better not to deal with this issue right now?

Did he deny the marriage wine just because his plan did not include an early start? Did he fail to heal those in need on the

Sabbath because the church might interpret it badly? Did he refuse to sit down with sinners because he would be associating with the wrong kind, and it would hurt the faith of the weak?

Avoidance and denial, compromise and appeasement, peacekeeping and diplomacy, or postponing to a more convenient time may not be options Jesus would have chosen. Whether we are sitting on the fence undecided, or fenced into opinions put on us by others, or standing outside the fence isolated by prejudice or even ignorance, it is time for a new vision for this field of battle. The fence is becoming a wall. If we do not find resolution soon, it may divide and destroy the ties that should bind us all together as family and, instead, leave us surrounded by the shambles of our brothers and sisters—those who have been outcasts long enough.

Arguing with God seeks to clarify the basic points of difference between antagonists. It appears the only solution to the dilemma of homosexuality requires arguing with others, with ourselves, and ultimately with that which each may perceive as God. Arguing, not fighting, could be the way home.

Acknowledgments

Several special people were instrumental in the creation of this book, though some suffered more than others during its development. Friends who live on both sides of this issue were continually in reach; in many conversations, letters, and e-mails, these people enabled me to explore more fragments of this complex problem. Alice and Les Dieter provided not only luminous insights, but also supported my work with intellectual hospitality and heartfelt interest. Several ministers, teachers, and social workers evoked questions and answers for the substance of these pages by sharing their points of view; however, because sometimes these good people are ahead of their congregations, clients, and peers in accepting gays, or behind them in still rejecting them, I will not name them, but I do thank them. Above all, without the constant prodding of my friend, Chuck, and the long suffering of my wife, Mary, and her insightful comments, support, and suggestions, as well as her editing assistance, the book would not exist. Thank you all.

INTRODUCTION

⁓

This is a dialogue about God, religion, bigotry, and Christianity. The catalyst for this dialogue is primarily homosexuality. The players are on opposite sides of the issue, and they will speak from the background of a long friendship.

Eli is a composite character, created from numerous, evangelical, fundamentalist Christians who believe the Bible is inerrant and is the last word on everything, including homosexuality. The character's arguments and statements in the dialogue are real, however—gleaned from common arguments, comments, letters, sermons, placards, and protest signs used by the religious fundamentalists of several faiths and denominations. Jay, on the other hand, is real and is a religious liberal who was at one time an evangelical, fundamentalist Christian.

Thanks to the foundation of a long-standing friendship, these two characters are able to avoid antagonism while offering honest and heartfelt arguments on controversial subjects. Eli holds a doctorate in theology from a conservative, Christian school and preaches at churches worldwide. Jay is an artist, writer, and educator and holds two degrees in liberal arts. Though he has been a searcher in theology for fifty years and reads widely in the subjects related to world religions, Jay claims no absolute theological answers and speaks as a layman.

The opinions included in this dialogue are, then, actual thoughts of various concerned individuals about a subject that increasingly requires new perspectives from the world. The homosexuality controversy has erupted in all societies, but it elicits enormously different reactions. Some areas of Africa have threatened men and women with death and imprisonment penalties just for being gay or aiding one who is. At the same time, on the streets of many American cities, gays parade openly every year in celebration of who they are. Unfortunately, it is also true that participants may risk verbal and physical attacks as they walk the same streets later.

Christianity and other religions play the role of biased referees in the competition for either the rights of or the elimination of the homosexual. The outcome of this competition is a significant issue not only to the homosexual, but to the world. This outcome also should be significant to those several religions that, in many ways, have built their houses on the discrimination of those who are different. Fundamentalist Christianity has said it even fears that if gay families were accepted, this recognition would bring about the end of civilization. More subtly, they also fear the diminishment of Christian credibility should homosexuality be deemed normal in the human race. Whether their adherents have built these houses of religion on a crumbling foundation of sand or whether they will remain upright through the truths to come is yet to be determined.

Any reader of *Arguing with God* will notice that one side of the argument is much longer and more detailed than the other. This is not a biased editing choice. The argument unfolds that way, plain and simple. There is a simple reason for this fact. The judgment about homosexuality from the fundamentalist faiths seldom allows an intellectual exchange. Instead, the reasoning of one side meets what is the equivalent of a prerecorded message from the other. The only argument the conservative fundamentalist presents in essence is, "God says so."

"Who says that God says so?" is the equally simple response to that prerecorded message. The faithful person then references some book or collection of books attributed to God. True, he or she admits that a man may have penned the book, but that man operated under the direct supervision of God. Thus, the writer defaults to God as the real author, and the human instrument equates a ghostwriter. If the other side then says, "Well, I don't believe that," that pretty well closes the debate. That is not a satisfactory stopping place, however, and it cheats all parties out of truth. And, in the case of the subject of *Arguing with God*, I am convinced it would be a mistake.

The dialogue is authentic, though it evolved from conversations with fundamentalist, conservative Christians from various parts of the world over many years of real debate. The composite character of Eli attempts to maintain the arresting tone and dialect of the lifelong Pentecostal Christian. As such, the word choice and sentence structure reflects a direct model of diction used by some in this group. It echoes the flavor of King James English from that version of the Bible. Even some of the word choices date to that book: "seemly" and "woeful" are good examples. Grammatical errors, or seasonings of speech, are actual diction examples from this religious community, and it seems at times that certain individuals often employ errors by design to signify humility or godliness.

Many gay Christians fear their homosexuality stamps them as inherently ungodly. This fear intensifies their alienation from God, and they feel they must hide who they are and deny their orientation, lest they succumb to what their church teaches them is temptation and sin. The few Bible verses that deal with homosexuality appear blatantly condemnatory and thus, on the surface, seem to support this judgment. The homosexual Christian often feels alone in his or her suffering, condemned by God, fellow believers, and even the general public—who legitimize hatred and prejudice through the church. This undoubtedly contributes to the inordinate number of gay suicides. It is an ultimate offense, then, when the Christian community has the audacity to use the high number of gay suicides to support their argument that being gay is innately disordered.

Further complicating the gay Christian's position is the fact that many fundamentalist believers have little comprehension of the realities involved in the gay person's life, and many even assume that one really chooses to be gay. There is no guarantee, but there is hope, that this book might assist each to understand the other a little better and start at least some on the road to happier relations. An equal desire is to offer healing to the gays, wounded by Christians, who struggle to see themselves as accepted and valued by God.

IN THE BEGINNING: THE ARGUMENTS

Jay: Not all Christian beliefs are the same, but some of those beliefs—simply *beliefs*, not necessarily facts, even—are awful. They affect people in enormous ways. It is those effects, the results of those beliefs, that make such beliefs so awful.

Eli: Awful? How do you mean?

Jay: Break the word apart. *Awful* means "full of awe"; think of "awesome," the word so overused today. But awesome has lost its effectiveness. If we rely on that word, "an awesome tidal wave" seems equal to "that awesome pair of socks in the window." *Awful* is inspirational or dreadful. The results of even your own Christian beliefs can be awful. They can be the motivation for a lifetime of charitable acts, but they are also the ground of tragic deaths.

Eli: Charitable acts, I see ... but what are the tragic deaths—martyrs or something like?

Jay: No, I am not referring to martyrs, though there are those. The tragic deaths, the awful results I mean, are those men and women, even teens, who are murdered or kill themselves because of some people's Christian beliefs.

Eli: There have been deaths over religion. Are you speaking of the Crusades, or what? And how do suicides come into this? I thought we were going to deal with a different issue today.

Jay: No, I don't mean the Crusades, although I am going to suggest that you are participating in a crusade even now, as a conservative, fundamentalist Christian. It is today's issue—gays and God—that is the catalyst for the awful results I mentioned. The fundamentalist's misunderstanding and condemnation of gays gives license to unbalanced people to attack gays, so we have violence and even murders. The mistaken condemnations of some Christians also foster self-hatred and suicide in young men and women who are already struggling in their turbulent adolescent years.

Eli: Now just how do we do that? I never purpose to send out killers into the world. I, and other Christians, simply preach the word.

Jay: By defining the gays as terrible sinners, even abominations, condemned by God, you, as a fundamentalist, create unintentionally tragic consequences. Not only do you identify the gays as righteous targets for others, but you pummel them psychologically through this condemnation of their very existence. These psychological wounds have consequences, especially on the young gays who do not have the tools to realize not all interpretations of God are correct. Thus, we see suicides. Hundreds, even thousands of them, are attributable to misguided religious interpretations.

Eli: Beliefs that you see as misguided and things that I see as wrong are going to be a bit different, I suspect. Well, that should supply us with fodder to chew on for a bit.

Jay: I expect so, too. The question will be whether we can lessen our differences. Some believers are firm in their ideas about God, and some are more flexible and allow for different interpretations of what or who God is.

Eli: Well, I am strong in my opinions, you might say. My faith tells me to simply accept the Word of God as my final authority. That is my opinion. So, how firm are you in your opinions?

Jay: My underlying opinions are solid, but I tend to follow more the attitude of Saint Augustine of Hippo. He pointed out, back in the fifth century, that what seems to separate God's creation of man from the animals is his ability to reason, and it would therefore be in error to deny reason and thoughtful interpretation when reading the Word of God. It would even be a sin to not use that reason in seeking God and the right.

I also admit to being stubborn, but I try to be open to new ideas. You have a wide ministry—preaching in churches on different sides of the world, even—and I know you encourage a strict view of the Bible and biblical Christianity. I want us to explore more of our beliefs and faith in our talks. Perhaps we could even share some articles and other people's opinions about Christianity and homosexuality. And I hope to find some common ground and some agreements as we talk and read. After all, we have known each other for, what, nearly fifty years now? That's a long time, though we fell out of touch.

Eli: Since you took off for the university and I took off for the army all those years ago, I have little doubt we will have many differences, even disagreements, to chew on. I am interested in what you picked up there. I already know you are not purely in harmony with much of what I deem to be truths, but I'm curious to know where you are now in the rest of your thinking.

Jay: And I see that after your army service, you acquired a doctorate. Congratulations.

You must have spent a lot of time at a university, too. I'm wondering if it was a liberal education or a more monologic education.

Eli: Monologic? Nice word—what does it mean? Is this one of those awful words like we talked about?

Jay: No, not awful. I just meant to ask whether your classes offered alternative points of view or facts that did not necessarily support what you already believed. Were they "one with your philosophy" already, or did the classes challenge your beliefs? Your opinions were already very strong in your early life, I recall.

Eli: I wasn't really at any university for all that long. Most of my classes were online and through correspondence. For the most part, though, they offered truths clearly stated in the Bible. But we also looked at a good number of the liberals' arguments. The world calls them Christian liberals, but I found what they had written to be, shall we say, arguable, if not totally weak. The Word of God is clear to all.

Jay: All right, let me start by asking a straightforward question that I think should throw us immediately into the middle of the subject of God and gays. Ready? A large number of the gays I know and hear about and read about either ask this question or at least think it.

The street preachers who harangue the participants attending many gay events or standing outside gay clubs say they want the gays to become Christians—evidently like the protesters are supposed to be. So, the question: why would any gay person wish to be a Christian when these Christians condemn them not just for what they do but even for who they are?

Eli: And I'm afraid I think that belief is nonsense. I have heard this line of reasoning before, and you have no doubt heard that Christians hate the sin, not the sinner.

Jay: Well, my friend, despite all the testimony to the contrary, far too many fundamentalist Christians appear to despise gay men and women for wanting, even needing, love—not to mention marriage. Heterosexual people take this sort of intimacy, this love and marriage, for granted, and the church is very happy to bless it while denying homosexuals the same thing. Perhaps, you do not see the church as hating the sinner, since you do not yet recognize that you degrade people for merely being who they are. Denying the very existence of these people, meaning people born gay—not choosing to be gay, notice—is a form of despising.

Eli: I know of the theory—gays feeling they are different ... not man ... not woman ... something else. Not! Even stupid people know this is not the case. Just the opposite is true. Everyone is the same; all are sinners. We don't hate anyone; we just condemn the actions.

Jay: I'm not at all sure that "even stupid people know," or even believe, everyone is the same. I'm guessing the preacher who travels around demonstrating and condemning and carrying signs bearing slogans like "God hates fags!" and "Matthew Shepard is in hell!" definitely hates who gay people are, not just what they do—so do all those in his congregation who travel with him (an entourage that consists mainly of his family, I understand). He is the poster child for Christianity to many who are born gay.

Now, are all Christians this blatant or mean? No. But hatred and discrimination can take many different forms, some more subtle than others. Telling a gay person that he only "thinks" he can't stand heterosexual contact, and that he just thinks he can only appreciate homosexual contact, is really a way of despising him—telling him he does not even exist the way he knows he does.

Now let's put this together a bit. Try to bear with me again. You seem to start from this assumption: gays are not who they think they are—meaning, gays are not people who are born homosexual. I assume you believe this because the Bible presents evidence that the authors of the Bible, at least, felt that God didn't want anything in his creation that didn't fit the "rule" of male or female—a logical response if you consider only part of the Bible.

Eli: Is evolution what you are hinting at here? Is that what is to be comprehended—or is your line of debate trying to make up a new sex?

Jay: I am not trying to make up a new sex—just as scientists do not make up new laws about the world, or the universe, or math, or chemicals. All humankind does is discover the wisdom or laws that are already there. One does not make the earth go around the sun by saying that it does or by discovering that it does. It just does. Joshua didn't make the sun stand still; he made (or God would have made) the earth stand still. We don't worry about that, and I can't really believe that anyone would feel it necessary to have to prove that the sun really stood still because that is what the Bible said. Or is there a deep theological reason we need to believe this is literally true instead of man's perception? It doesn't change God or who he is either way, does it?

Let us then move to a place you really may not be able to go or even think about. If you can't, you can't. At least my talking about it helps to clarify it for me, as I have to discover all these things as I grow. We know that the animal and even the plant kingdoms have varieties of sexuality or ways of reproducing. Some animals are both sexes and fertilize themselves; even the cellular animals that have the gift of life, like the amoeba, reproduce asexually, if I remember my biology. Some sharks will actually change their sex from male to female or female to male if there is a shortage of that gender in the environment. It allows for continual reproduction. How they do this or how they know to do this is totally beyond me.

What humans call homosexuality has been with the race since language. Men have perceived it differently in different eras, but it is there. History is replete with examples: Gilgamesh and Enkidu; Achilles and Patroclus; the Greek, Roman, and Egyptian societies; and aboriginal Americans—one of the cultures that valued the gays instead of ostracizing them.

The Native Americans even honored those born homosexual, calling them the two-spirited people. So, you see, I am not creating a new sex; I and others in contemporary society are now beginning to understand not a new variety of human, but a variety that was always there. We simply did not completely recognize this variation present in human beings' sexual orientation for what it is. We have only recently begun to grasp the multiplicity and complexity of people's sexuality. Our increasing comprehension is a parallel of our continually growing understanding of physiology as we search even the DNA and the genetic makeup of living organisms.

The early biblical writers may not have been in error in condemning what they then perceived as homosexual activity; some of the activity it refers to was harmful. But we too often take the Bible to mean what it never intended to mean. True, homosexuality is not the dominant sexual orientation in a species, though I believe the percentage is a bit larger than has been the going statistic since Kinsey. Even I am shocked at the large number of married men who are now living and dying in a marriage they undertook because society expected it of them and, in many cases, because they couldn't accept their sexuality. I can name seven or eight men right in my town without much reflection. They are not "new" gays—just finally admitting it to others, as well as to themselves, at times.

What's more, as you point out, gays do not go out and fill the earth with their seed, or reproduce (actually, they do, but not with one another). Thus they are not following the command to replenish the earth, I guess. Of course, that isn't really a commandment, is it? If you take it literally, maybe we should take literally that man should earn his bread by the sweat of his brow, which would pretty much condemn businessmen and -women, most teachers and preachers, and all the office workers. Are we supposed to work up a sweat when we preach?

So, we can understand the biblical writers when they condemn homosexuals. This orientation is not the norm; it is not the most visible human condition, and many people didn't and don't even know that they are gay. Do the biblical writers understand the complete man? Don't tell me, "Maybe not, but God did, and he dictated the Bible." He also understood the cosmic relationships, but that did not interfere with the sun's standing still in the sky for Joshua. The concept of replenishing the earth—fertility, if you will—was a monstrously huge principle in ancient religions. Think of Osiris, Dionysus, the sacrifices of Aztecs or Mayas for crops, and so on. Fertility is necessary for survival not only for crops, but for the tribal warriors as well.

There is no reason for us to assume the Bible covers everything that is a part of creation. It does not deal with the concept of higher math or quantum physics or even the birth and death of stars or the speed of light, at least directly. Psychologists and physicists and geologists are not creating new laws, even though when they discover one, it is often named after them. But Newton didn't invent gravity; he just defined it a bit. The Bible even uses the length of a day metaphorically. Remember, a thousand years is as a day with God.[ii] Why do we have to assume the creation was in twenty-four-hour days, or even in one-thousand-year days?

Eli: Do we all need and want love? Certainly, but unmarried, Christian men and women, no matter how much they want love and intimacy, know fornication is out—nada! But you say the homosexual says, "I am different ... I need sex prior to marriage." According to the Bible, premarital sex can't happen!

Jay: Aye, there's the rub. "Fornication is out; I need sex prior to marriage," you say. But, for gays, there is no marriage, remember? You who deplore gay sex and marriage are the ones who compel them to break your rules. All people want and need love and intimacy, you say, yet you disallow sex before marriage or outside of marriage, and then you try to forbid gays to marry. I know; I can hear your argument: "They can marry, just not homosexually." But if they marry heterosexually, for most, that intimacy is at best just mutual masturbation while they fantasize the sex they really want and need. And we all know that sinning in thought is still sin, isn't it? Thus, marriage becomes a lie!

Ask yourself this: did I, as your loved friend, meet your need for love and intimacy? Of course not. Did you enjoy my company? At times. Now, consider how this compares to the life of a gay person who is married heterosexually. One side of the partnership is "in love"; the other is trying to meet expectations beyond what he or she is able to feel, even though they most always desperately wish to feel that way.

Eli: God understands! Certainly he does. Figure a way! The gay way is the wrong way. Say I love my neighbor's wife ... so what? I leave her alone! Or I love my buddy and want to have an interlude at the back of the rest area along the interstate—nope, can't do it! Is this hate? Not on your life, unless being against other forms of vice is hate—like being against drunk drivers is hate ... you know, the drunkards who cannot help themselves. They just need a hit in the morning, and at noon, and then again before the evening meal ... and at night.

Jay: "Figure a way," you say. How simple. You see it as, "Just figure a way to not fall to temptation." But that ignores the basic and larger problem—that is, how to fulfill the self that exists, just as the heterosexuals fulfill their desires. The parallel you should use is that the gay man should be happy with his one partner and not look across the fence to his gay neighbor's handsome partner. That would be more of an equal comparison.

Now, the drunkard (could we say alcoholic?) cannot help himself, because he is an alcoholic. It is a genetic problem. In that sense, I will accept comparison to homosexuality, as I believe the latter is probably genetic, too. But the alcoholic has to consume alcohol for his alcoholism to even come into play in his life. The homosexual is simply homosexual. He or she knows it because it is part of the very makeup of the personality; it is the I, the me, the self. Homosexuality is inseparable from the person.

The first thing the physician says to the mother at the birth of the baby is either "It's a girl!" or "It's a boy!" That refers to the whole child, really—not just the reproductive organs. When the parent hears the sex of the child, she envisions not the organ, but the clothing, the room, the games the growing child will play. The parent knows which life to prepare the child to live.

But—and this is a big but—that image is not always true and never has been the whole truth. That gender image has forced literally millions of children into a mold that was not made for them. Some even survived this arbitrary assignment; far too many did not. Those who did survive often were warped and bent into creatures that preyed on others. Some took the pain and isolation inherent in this unrecognized and often hidden difference and turned it to creativity in the arts. Some could not and just suffered silently and alone, ignorant of any remedy.

People have nearly always accepted an overly simplistic definition of gender. Only today, other than earlier, isolated incidents like with the Native Americans, are we trying to understand scientifically the multiple orientations of men and women. Some are only attracted to their own genders, others only to the opposite, but most have degrees of attraction to both sexes.

The alcoholic more correctly compares to one who is allergic to a certain food, like peanuts or broccoli. The alcoholic can live without drinking and still not deny himself or herself a full and rich life, just as the one who cannot eat peanuts can live a full life without them. But the person born gay cannot simply avoid being gay. Homosexuality is not a reaction to an outside agent; it is the inside; it is the person; homosexuality is not an agent at all. So, I will not accept the comparison.

The guy who loves his neighbor's wife ... well, it happens a lot, I know. Is it right? No. Is this the same problem as homosexuality? Not really, but I should clarify a bit here. A gay might fall to this vice the same way a straight person could. Homosexuals do marry each other and truly love their partners. They are then liable to the same problems as straight marriages. They cheat, break each other's hearts, and divorce. In this sense, homosexuality can include the vice of coveting your neighbor's wife, but it is not coveting that we are discussing here.

Nor is homosexuality the same as the vice you intimate with "I want to have sex with my buddy on the interstate." Many of those incidents may occur, but so do interludes, as you label them, that last fifty years—between committed couples in their homes, not in dark parks or at rest stops. The notion of homosexual activity occurring primarily at disreputable locations assumes all gay sex is nefarious. Gays also live in good neighborhoods and attend family gatherings. There are lesbian couples living next door to me and across the street from me right now. They never go to the rest areas for interludes. Need I say more on this false accusation? One cannot define homosexuality as a vice. Vices are actions; homosexuality is a state of being; and, just like straight people, gays seek to achieve full and rich lives. I see this differing viewpoint as a crux of the problem between you and me, and between gays and some religious sects.

Eli: Do we Christians feel for these mentioned? Certainly, and we are reaching to aid. But to say, as you seem to, that these gays were born that way and there is no change in store for them … well …

Jay: They *are* born that way! There is no change in store for them. They will always be gay or lesbian. Could God change them? Sure, if he were God and wanted to change them. But why would he want to? Unlike Paul, he is not all that caught up in sex in the first place. It doesn't even exist in heaven: we will be as the angels, neither marrying nor giving in marriage, according to the Bible.[iii] Instead, we will all be one, yet separate, sort of like the Trinity. He does not have to follow the rules in the Bible even if there are people who believe the text is all there is to him and that the biblical authors knew him better than anyone else.

Eli: That flies in the face of "all have sinned and come short of the glory of God … the gift of God is eternal life…" Do all men and women battle with habits and conflicts hidden from others? They probably all do. That is a statement of scripture: all have come short. That is why Jesus came: not to leave us in the ditch, but to get us out.

Jay: You seem to be starting from the proposition that being homosexual is a sin that one commits, not a trait that one is born with. It is difficult to fall short of the glory, as the Bible says, if one starts short. Of course all sin—gays, too.

We again are in the position of condemning gays for not having one single mate; the world denies them that opportunity and yet condemns them for promiscuity. You and the straight world skip the elephant in the room—that the *only* intimacy the gay enjoys or can even tolerate is not heterosexual. There is no "waiting for marriage" or "waiting for the right girl or guy." There will never be a marriage or the right one in the sense of a heterosexual relationship.

The only option you leave to these millions of people is, "Well, tough. God said it's not good for man to be alone, but he did not mean it in your case."[iv] In the case of the gays, there is not going to be a future wife or husband whom they can love romantically. There is no outlet for their sexuality. And if you say that they could still get married and have sex with the "proper" mate, think of it like this. Just imagine a future wherein you, yourself, in order to be a good Christian man, citizen, or whatever, have to marry another man and have sex only with him. This in essence is what you are asking the gays to do. How satisfying would that be? Wouldn't you say, "But I am not that way! I was born straight! How am I supposed to meet your expectations? I can't!"

Or, if homosexuality were the command of the deity in this imaginary universe, and God condemned heterosexism in passages parallel to those in which the Bible condemns homosexuality in our universe, how would you deal with it? Think about it. Think about it!

Eli: The church is a place for many people who need help, prayer, and consolation. We help each other. But we don't let a fellow say, "I have the okay of God to do the adultery thing, because I was born that way." It does not compute. There is a list of things that God has not been pleased with for ages—fornication, adultery, stealing, murder—and the thing is that Jesus took all our sin on himself to set us free from the grip of these and other sins.

Jay: I sometimes wonder about the accuracy of that biblical statement. I know of no people set free from the grip of these and other sins. Sin continually tempts all of my friends and yours. If they refused to fall to temptation, one could say, "They are set free," I suppose, but what does one say when they, like Paul, still do that which they hate?[v] In what way are they set free from the grip of these? The Bible does not say they are set free from the punishment for these, though that is what we accept subjectively and in a connotative sense.

Eli: I read an article proposing the honoring of gay and lesbian victims of the Nazis with a monument in Berlin. How inappropriate can something be? How about putting the memorial out there for the 800,000 Christians killed by the Nazis, as exposed in the May 1940 issue of Time *magazine?*

Jay: I'm afraid I miss your point about being inappropriate. There were Jews, Christians, Muslims, and atheists killed, too. Such a monument would just be about the gays history often ignores. They wore the pink triangle, not the yellow star. The Nazis killed them because they were gay; I'm not sure they killed the Christians because they were Christian. Most of the gays were probably Christian, too.

Is it wrong to remember the gays killed because of who they were, not what they did—just who they were? I see nothing wrong with honoring the Christian or the Jews killed as well, but there is enough honor to go around, isn't there? Or is it all held tightly in some selfish or self-righteous fist?

Eli: First, I am a Christian, bigot and all. I am tolerant even of the intolerant who are intolerant to the Christian and his Bible. As a Christian, I am pressing for transformation to the mind of Christ. Christ really thinks he is the final judge, and his character is the object of a singular goal: eternal life.

Is homosexuality a religion, a race? I know of many black pastors who are enraged that they are linked to the battle for the homosexuals, and rightly so. Race is an act of God. Homosexuality is a choice. The decisions and actions of such a lifestyle amount to disobedience, lawlessness, and self-will, guaranteed.

The actions of the flesh, as stated in Galatians 5, are not approved or tolerated by God. He is intolerant of what he does not like or approve. Dads are like that. Some things are not dealt with in scripture, so they are at times appropriate and other times not: wearing a necktie at a presidential dinner, cutting one's hair into a blue and yellow Mohawk, and so on. Picking one's nose in the pulpit is not sin … just dumb.

Some things are really an abomination to the Boss: bearing false witness against one's neighbor, breaking a covenant, taking the neighbor's wife as if she were for yourself. There are a lot of things "Dad" does not like. And he said that when he comes, he will deal with matters. (I remember Mom telling me she was going to tell Dad about my misbehaviors when he came home. Angst!)

I don't see denying gays a memorial as being selfish. When are we going to start putting up memorials for the drunkards who fought in the war, or the liars who lied us into victory, or the murderers who slaughtered hundreds for the cause? If they fought and gave their lives for the battle, let's honor them for giving their all, not for being an alcoholic or … you get the point. What shall we teach the generations coming? That is not being selfish, is it?

The Dying Church: Positive versus Negative Christianity

Jay: You seem to have a rather unique definition of *selfish*. I recall, when we were talking earlier, you asked for definitions of a few words. Maybe, just to be safe, I had better offer some ideas on their meanings in the context of the article we were talking about, "A Loss of Faith," by Michael Hampson.[vi] As I recall, Hampson comments that a new, non-Anglican, evangelical fundamentalism has tragically altered the heretofore, blessedly liberal traditions of the Church of England.

We need to start with the concept of *denotation* and *connotation* first, of course. The denotation is the most objective meaning possible, the one you would find in the dictionary, and the connotation includes the nuances of emotional and subjective responses innate in all language. The notion of connotation acknowledges that time also changes the meanings of words (or at least how individuals define them), as does social position, education level, and even one's mood at a given time. The speaker or writer may, and most often does, have a slightly different definition of a word he uses than does his reader or listener.

For example, if you use the word *gay* in the pulpit, the congregants will have one general idea of who you mean, but most everyone will have a different emotional response to the word. Some will experience fear, for themselves or their children. Some will feel anger and hatred—righteous hatred, no doubt. Others will experience shame as they peek out of the corners of their eyes and wonder if the brother and sister sitting next to them have any idea that they are gay. Some will experience sorrow, since they have known some gay people in their lives and loved them but just couldn't continue to associate with them, since the gay is an abomination to their loving God. Others will simply feel confused, having no concept of what a gay person really is and mistakenly associating homosexuality with pedophilia, since they have heard of that connection from certain preachers who believe that out of ignorance.

Now, we need to realize that all this rhetoric is not simply a form of relativism. Language, at least the English tongue, is living. That means it changes with usage, unlike Latin, called a dead language, as no one uses it anymore as a primary, vulgar tongue. That is why we use it in sciences and law to define terms we want to keep constant.

Again, I believe all of your requested definitions came from the statement in Hampson's article that evangelical fundamentalism has destroyed a four-hundred-year-old, liberal, Anglican tradition in only twenty years. As such, I think you are primarily interested in the words *liberal*, *fundamentalism*, *gay*, and some interrelated terms, so I will answer within that context (as context also changes definitions).

Liberal has mostly a dictionary definition—that is, open-minded, generous, and willing to listen and learn from others, as opposed to being closed-minded and bearing the banner of "my mind is made up; don't confuse me with the facts."

Politically, this contrasts with conservatives, and this contrast is connotative, because the political conservatives have left behind the old definition of *conservative*. The new definition seems to me to incorporate and practice the concepts of greed, selfishness, and bigotry. It is almost more like the Objectivist philosophy espoused by Ayn Rand than the original conservative philosophy of the GOP.

But let me get back to the point. Theologically I use the term liberal to label those who have an open-minded approach to religion. They are willing to listen to new findings and new studies. They tend to practice the social gospel of loving others as they love themselves, instead of condemning others as they condemn themselves—the practice too often found in the fundamentalist churches. (This is really an interesting phenomenon that will bear further discussion, I'm sure.) The definition of *fundamentalism* is necessary now.

Fundamentalism, as used in Hampson's article, carries the denotation of a belief system that attaches completely to the fundamental elements of a particular religion or philosophy. In this particular case, fundamentalists are those who take literally the biblical writings and do not attach any significance to the possibility of metaphor, hyperbole, simile, poetic license, myth, or even an author's individual and potentially incorrect perspective.

Fundamentalists accept the Bible as inerrant, as the Catholics accept the pope as inerrant (in most cases). They take everything literally—including the creation story. Indeed, they even feel that taking the creation story at face value as scientific truth is essential for them to get into heaven. That seems to be because the Bible, or at least the King James Version, is to be treated with a reverence almost equal to that given to God or Jesus. Thus, if the Bible displayed any errors or untruths, its inerrancy would be in question, and where would that lead? If any part were wrong, it might all be wrong!

Therefore, the fundamentalists Hampson refers to would accept any biblical verses against effeminate humans (though not lesbians during the Old Testament period at least) as God's word and not open to question. In contrast, the liberal would say there might be a chance that the author of that or another Bible verse could be wrong, operating from his own time and understanding. The fundamentalist says if it is written, it is right, no matter what.

The word *alien* in the quote means "foreign," as in "not British." Connotatively it also carries the hope that the English people, and especially the Anglicans, whose ancestors started the protestant Church of England in the time of Henry VIII, will realize their great, liberal history (including running to the colonies to be able to follow their beliefs) and recognize that the huge protests against the gay human beings that God created are being fueled by foreign churches that bear the Anglican name. The alien fundamentalists in this case are in Africa. They object to gay priests, gay marriage, gay people (who they have said do not exist in Africa), and most of them object to female priests, female bishops, and females having rights in general. They too often do not object to genocide or social decay in their own societies, though.

The whole quotation from the article is an unhappy statement with an edge of nationalist feelings. The author is saying that the grand, old, historical Church of England is losing its claim to social justice and intellectual justice and freedom. Ironically, it is the descendants of those native Africans, proselytized by the missionaries—the same missionaries who originally carried the gospel to Africa to save the natives from their darkness—who are pushing this slide into fundamentalism.

The article is saying that while the home country in Europe continued to evolve into a more enlightened state, much of the African church remains rooted in literal fundamentalism. There is a further possibility that the author is referring to the United States in the "alien" context, since the United States likewise houses some of the radical fundamentalists. By the way, the word *radical* would carry the meaning of "over the edge," or at the very extreme of whatever it was modifying—so, radicals are those who really, strongly believe in literalism.

Eli: I will accept these definitions for now. I also read recently about the failure of Christianity in Holland—that few people bother with church now. I wonder if the liberal church not preaching truth any longer causes this disinterest.

Jay: Actually, I have thought about this phenomenon, this diminishment, of Christianity in Holland and in much of Europe. Is it liberalizing that did it, or was it the church's failure to grow in understanding of God as people grew in understanding of themselves and their world? Is the church becoming irrelevant because it refuses to follow common sense and persists in its limited understanding of the past? In other words, are people still exorcising demons when the patient needs penicillin? One does not convert others by telling them how bad they are. Everyone is bad.

I believe that God is even now using the schism in the Episcopal and the Anglican Communions to move us another step toward truth. Just as when people saw slavery for what it was and abolished it in many places, and when women finally realized their rights, mankind is beginning to realize that God's purpose continues to encompass all, even those formerly despised. Monarchy gave way to democracy, and as monarchist clergy faded in the protestant realms, we began to recognize the image of God in all of us, and that the commandments written on our hearts, instead of in stone, were commands of "Thou shalt!" instead of "Thou shalt not!"

We begin to grasp that if we are to be like him, we must concentrate on the beauty of each other, not the blackness. We understand that darkness is just the absence of light, and if we bring light, all is well, and all is right. We do not need to pull the mote out of our brother's eye. He and God will do that. It is not ours to judge. Judgment comes from within, and even then the Bible says if we condemn ourselves, there is one greater than our hearts that says, "neither do I condemn you."[vii]

I saw and heard a fundamentalist preacher with a megaphone at a gay parade the other day. He was screaming, "You are ugly! You think you are beautiful, but you are really filth! God judges you an abomination, and you will burn for eternity!" Absolutely nobody, either in the parade or watching the parade, felt the need to change who they were. Instead, the crowd looked on in disbelief at the hatred coming from this man. Today, instead of the biblical saying that they will know you are Christians by your love, too often, they know you are Christians by your hate.[viii]

It seems to me that one ought to emphasize the positive, not the negative. Preachers should be smiling, not scowling. Their fingers should not be jabbing at those they profess to love, lest the objects of their ire become discouraged and leave. Instead, the fingers should be reaching out to embrace. Think how different the message would be if it were, "I am concerned about you. I know you are lonely and even in pain at times, like all of us. How can I help you?" This seems to echo more strongly the intent of the biblical words of Jesus telling those who are heavily laden to come to him, and he will give them rest.[ix]

Eli: I agree; I once saw a sign put up for the congregation of a church, "A fake smile is better than genuine depression. Smile!" It helped the levity of the church meetings, and it opened a door to many comments.

Jay: It is the nature of man to be lonely. The Europeans, even with their freedom and liberality, are lonely, too. When God is offered to fill the loneliness and to bring meaning, he is accepted more readily than when he is presented only as the judge and executioner. It seems to me the good news is that God has provided a defense attorney, too.

THE THREAT OF ANGLICAN-EPISCOPAL SCHISM

Eli: I am a bigot, biased and prejudiced; remember? When we get to heaven, no doubt we will discover the shocking reality that it is a closed system. There is only one name under heaven, remember, whereby we must be saved.ˣ Yes, I am on one side—without argument. On this earth, there is much reasoning put forth by many, from evolutionists to creationists. Each one is probably thinking he is broad-minded and a genius in his own eyes.

I recall the scripture saying there is more hope for a fool than one who thinks he is wise … so humility goes a long way, even in Mosaic faith and Christianity. I find it hilarious that most who oppose Christians try to put us into the stereotype of reading scripture all day long and not looking into anything called research, science, or even liberal arts. It is noteworthy to me that those we see as bigoted and narrow-minded often accuse us of bigotry and narrow-mindedness. But that is the way it is supposed to be in mind wars and in physical/political wars.

Jay: You know, I'm beginning to think you are mistaken in saying you are a bigot and closed-minded. In the next sentence or so, you then say you like science and the empirical system. That indicates that you are open to discovery. I think I understand why you claim to be a bigot. It would be an effective salve for those who feel picked on for being bigoted Christians by offering a way to respond to their critics. Instead of disproving that one is closed-minded or a bigot, one would just take pride in being one, because that is what God would want. It is sort of a way to avoid the real questions, though.

Eli: And what are the real questions? Everyone I meet is a thinker. They are not about to tell me they are stupid! So, they have a dug-in belief that is, in my opinion, wrong! *Being a dyed-in-the-wool, Bible-thumpin' believer, I take joy in seeing the expressions on the faces of those confronted with other ideas. Remember my old dictionary, the one by Funk and Wagnalls, published in the 1890 era? The definition for bigot: "anyone who will not change his opinion and actions no matter how much presentation given to the contrary"! And it goes on to say, by a French commentator, that the worst kind of bigot is one who is convinced he is not one. So, I am a Christian. I am convinced he is the only way of salvation. We would know nothing of him but for the Bible—the library of books written by forty-four authors over fourteen hundred years on three continents ... with one message and purpose ... to reveal the life and desire of the almighty God for his creation, mankind.*

I am proud to be a bigot, prejudiced, biased ... by the Word of God. Those freeze words used in college, university, and seminary I attended are not freezing anymore. We are all guilty of being those ... just some think that Christians should run to the corner, get out of the public forum, and leave it all to them.

Jay: I understand faith and trust, to some extent, but I don't make my faith say there is only one way to interpret and understand, or I would be untrue to my faith, which tells me to think as well as to have faith.

Eli: How does that fare with Christ saying he is the only begotten of the Father, the Way, Truth and Life? "No man comes unto the Father but by me"—how does that fare with the many religions of Zoroastrianism, Buddhism, Hinduism, Mormonism, and Jehovah's Witnesses? Do all roads lead to truth—to God, to heaven?

Jay: My faith says God has, or even is, the attribute of truth. I would not fear seeking the truth, because the truth, whatever it may do to former beliefs, can only lead to God. It is not a matter of pride, of intelligence, or of learning; it is an attitude of accepting that I do not and cannot know or understand all of the mechanisms of the universe, physically or spiritually. I let God take care of that; he didn't assign me that job.

Eli: He has assigned to us the job of being like him: creative; truth-seeking; knowing the difference between error and truth; accepting and embracing truth and rejecting deception; and giving warning to those who are on the road to destruction.

Jay: He assigned me to love my brother as myself, to not judge, and to see Jesus in all men; whatsoever I do to the least of these, I do to him.

Eli: Now this is interesting. Does loving my brother mean warning him of the wrath to come? Jesus said yes. Tell him of the Good News, for those who believe and obey the gospel … will have eternal life. Does not judging mean not condemning? Not warning? Not displaying the light through the cracks?

Judging sour and sweet, dirty and clean, light and dark … is the duty of the sane. Walking in darkness is disliked by all the holy writings. To use holy writings to make me look better or more righteous … now, that is not to be done. But to say to people that they are wrong when they

are wrong is good and acceptable judgment that God and his writers
display all over the Word.[1]

---

1   The act of judging is mentioned very freely and very emotionally in the arguments concerning God and homosexuality, but the point that Eli just made demonstrates a difficulty that debaters on all sides too often ignore at the cost of throwing the argument off track. One meaning of the word refers to the duty of the magistrate (or even just to the magistrate) who sits in judgment of another *person*—to pronounce one guilty or innocent, to forgive or to condemn, or even to set the punishment. Another meaning, though related, is not really the same. To judge whether something is wise or foolish, valid or invalid, or even right or wrong carries the meaning of *assessing*, and this is not quite the same thing. In this sense (assessing), people on both sides of the debate, liberal or conservative, continually make judgments. It would be difficult to live without doing so. The problem is that Eli loads his argument with the assessment definition to shoot down Jay's magistrate argument—that one should not sit in God's place, deciding whether a man's actions merit a certain fate. This means that Eli and Jay are actually arguing different points. The argument is duplicitous.

Judging carries emotional baggage, and the slur, "Judge not!" which gays and their supporters hurl at fundamentalist Christians, may not be entirely fair or accurate. The intention is to use the Bible against the Bible. The specific reference for this judging is usually the first verse of Matthew, chapter 7. But, throughout the Bible, everyone is exhorted to judge, to *assess* right and wrong. This is what many Christian fundamentalists are attempting to do. They should not be condemned for this. It does not make sense to tell Christians they shouldn't attempt to assess or judge what is right and wrong—that is one of the goals of the faith. It is when this assessment then leaps the huge chasm, which it most always does, and the person takes on the power and authority of the magistrate who makes the ultimate decision about another person, that one can say, "Judge not!"

Also, what is left out of this biblical reference is the second part of the admonition to not judge found in the following verses of the same chapter—that one risks being judged in the same manner using an equal measuring device by an even greater magistrate. This rather indicates it is perfectly all right to judge another if one is indeed in a state of perfection and need not fear being judged in turn. Of course, one then must balance one's perfection in a larger context as well. The judgment quote is found in what is referred to as the Sermon on the Mount, which runs from chapter 5 through chapter 7 in Matthew. One of the earlier lessons in the sermon is that a hunger for a sinful gratification is as much a sin as committing the sin itself. This makes it enormously more difficult for one to find oneself perfect enough to be able to condemn others without risk of being condemned oneself.

The gay supporters must try to differentiate the fundamentalists who carry signs pronouncing judgment and condemnation of a person from those assessing the morality of an action. The Christian, gay or straight, must assess the morality of an action, but the Bible admonishes the Christian against condemning or even determining the guilt or moral status of a person other than himself or herself.

Jay: Well, just loving my brother takes most of my time and energy. I often counsel gays who feel trodden upon by the church sometimes, and the pain felt by the gay community is great. Because civil laws and much religious dogma discriminate against them, gays understand clearly that many people and most fundamental religions do not accept them. Because the Bible condemns them, with the Old Testament calling them an abomination and the New Testament somewhat bizarrely suggesting that being gay is a punishment for not worshipping God in the right way, Christian gays inevitably wrestle with the idea they were born despised by God.

This rejection often comes out in anger or even in sexual excesses, because gay people learn to hate themselves, as they see the rest of the world doing. Drug and alcohol abuse, suicide, and outrageous acts in public could be a way to sort of spit in the enemy's face. I suspect gays often do not realize why they do these things; they assume it is just part of being gay.

Eli: I am aware of the self-hatred. I am aware of the deception of it. Are gay people loved by Jesus? Yes! By the Father? Yes. Accepted as humans? Yes. Left to continue in this lifestyle? No. Gossipers are not left there. Angry men are not left there. Drunkards, adulterers, haters of father and mother, and covenant breakers are not left there. This you were, said Paul, but now you are washed, clean and fit for the master's use.

Jay: Equating being gay with being a gossiper, drunk, adulterer, or hater is ignoring the question. It simply skips my argument that the Bible is not the literal, inerrant mind of God and is a product of men of a particular time and cultural setting. As such, we must interpret the instances of the Bible's "gay bashing," if you would, in the same manner we ignore the Bible's permission in Exodus 21:7 to sell one's daughter into slavery. We ignore the permission in Leviticus 25:44 to own slaves if they are from another nation. We dismiss Leviticus 11:10 that eating shellfish is an abomination. We no longer feel as Leviticus 11:6 through 11:8 does, that God forbids us to eat or even touch a dead pig; nor do we grant that the woman raped in the fields is possibly innocent, while the woman raped in the town probably wanted it, or she would have cried out for help, as is described (along with other interesting sexual behavior) in chapter 22 of Deuteronomy.

Look at what the Bible implies when differentiating the rapes in town versus the rapes in a field. The purpose is that sometimes the man may be innocent and accused wrongly. It says that the woman could lie. The text grants that if she was raped in the field, she couldn't help it, but it does not mention the reservation that she could have been a willing accomplice or even instigator in the field as well. It seems evident to me we should consider the spirit of the law—not just conclude that the field equals life and the town brings death.

The same is true for the biblical references to homosexuality. Notice how we all jump so readily to the sin of Sodom and Gomorrah being homosexuality. Look closely at the story related in Genesis chapters 18 and 19. First the story presents Abraham as a clever man bargaining with God to spare the cities if even ten good men are to be found in them. He has to remind the Lord that he is a good God. Does this scenario seem likely? Does God need reminding?

The cities are likewise going to be destroyed for the sins they had committed prior to the visit of the angels. We do not know what these sins were. They may or may not have been sexual. Each of the cities in the plain and surrounding areas had its own ruler. They warred against each other and formed alliances. One of the methods employed throughout man's violent warlike past to demonstrate dominance over the conquered enemy is sexual domination—rape, by men and women.

The law of hospitality—which includes not just guidelines for good manners, but the full protection of one's guests—toward those taken into one's household represents a sacred obligation. Lot has persuaded the angels to be his guests; he is responsible for them. Then, all the men of the city come to rape them. Notice this is *all* the men of the city. Are all the men of the city gay, even the men engaged to Lot's two daughters? Is this likely? All the males are gay and want to carry out their lust on the two strangers? This appears more to be straight men wanting to show dominance over the strangers from another kingdom (surely these men did not know the guests were all powerful angels). What we understand today to be homosexuals or gays are not straight men and women who are acting out of lust or a wish for dominance over same-sex partners. Those we label as gay today are only attracted homosexually, and the attraction results in an emotional attachment as well as sexual. Gays are not advocating breaking the laws of the sacredness of guests and hospitality.

This, further, does not seem pointed at sexual sin, since Lot offers his virgin daughters to be gang-raped—or whatever the men choose to do with them. Gang rape would be a sexual sin as well. If we grant that not all of the men of the city were gay, such men would have displayed a preference for female virgins, if men were men as they are today. But the gang does not want sex. They want to show their dominance over the strangers, it seems. Even the story in Genesis 19:8 has Lot trying to dissuade the gang of men by saying, "… only unto these men do nothing; for therefore came they under the shadow of my roof."

One wonders how righteous the daughters were who safely came out of the city. Later they violate their father, commit incest with him, and bear children from him. If God was destroying the cities for not being righteous, it seems rather arbitrary to play favorites with anyone. God likewise offered the men engaged to Lot's daughters escape from the coming destruction, yet they had to have been a part of the mob; the Bible says the mob was all the men, from all sections of the city. One wonders about these men's feelings when seeing their future wives offered this way. This story raises too many questions to be a simple statement of God destroying a plain of cities (not just the two) because of the homosexuality that wasn't even what we know homosexuality to be today.

Judges, chapter 19, is almost a parallel of the story of Sodom. It tells of the sins of the tribe of Benjamin. A mob in the town of Gibeah demanded a host send out a protected guest—a man, as in Sodom—so the men of the town could rape and abuse him. Again, the host offered his own virgin daughter in place of the guest, as well as the guest's concubine, to be done with as the crowd sees fit. (Women do not seem to find much chivalry from the ancient Jews, do they?) The mob finally did gang rape the concubine, and she died on the doorstep after the mob finished with her. The other tribes of Israelites then joined in war and almost wiped the tribe of Benjamin off the map for this crime. Note it was not for homosexuality but, rather, for denying hospitality, perhaps even human decency, that God ostensibly leads the Israelites in the deaths of the men and women of this town and the near extinction of the tribe of Benjamin. This parallel story and what follows is definitely unpleasant, but significant, when considering the account of Sodom and Gomorrah in Genesis.

It seems inherently obvious that many laws or admonitions were products of a particular culture, age, and mind-set. Likewise, contemporary society perceives the gay question in an entirely different perspective scientifically, medically, and even theologically in many denominations. Now, unlike in Old Testament ages, priests can "approach the altar" even if they are not perfect specimens physically, or if they wear glasses.[xi]

Even the fact that many gays choose to live their lives in the closet, denying who they really are and living a life of deception, can stand as testimony to the lie that one chooses to be gay. If gays had chosen to be gay, why on earth would they hide it? It is blatantly illogical! Being gay is not the same as being a child molester, or a murderer, or an adulterer. One *becomes* those things through choices. One does not choose to be gay; one simply *is*.

Eli: I disagree. One is what God says he is. Self-deception has to face the music of the character of Christ. He is the goal. Self-hatred is a normal, human thing. Who has not fought that dragon? It is a good fight.

Recall, there is no temptation that has taken you but such as is common to man—is common![xii] *"But," they say, "I don't want to be common ... I am special." And that is true: each person is one of a kind—one with an eternal purpose in the providence of God.*

Jay: I agree that the gay person may be one of a kind—one who, because of who he is, may bring completion and joy to another gay who would otherwise have lived an empty life if he had denied who he is. Gays may exist for others' completion and joy as well; it is not good for man to be alone, remember? I am not at all convinced that homosexuality is a temptation, but if it is, it certainly is not common to man, as you say. A gay man or woman could choose to deceive the world and pretend to be straight, but they never would be heterosexual. Simply put, homosexuality is *not* a common temptation they are dealing with.

Eli: One does *choose to be* gay. *Happy is a good thing. Don't confuse the word anymore. Make it a battle of offensiveness. Become like Christ. Homosexual is not the way any person is born. To give in to the compulsion to act, to make a habit of it ... to say "I can't quit, so it must be normal"—that approach could be taken in voyeurism ... in lust ... or in any human battle.*

Jay: You cannot accomplish anything in a discussion of the issue by redefining the word *gay*. Declaring the word to have only its older meaning and denying its present use as a term for "homosexual" doesn't work. Just because one can choose to be happy has nothing to do with whether one can choose to be gay. That disingenuous argument ignores the real question. Nevertheless, we come back to the same issue: the literal acceptance of the Bible's words. Does "God-breathed," as the Bible has been described, mean "inspired by the spirit of God," with the writer consciously participating, thus bringing in his vision as an instrument of God, or does it mean the man's brain had absolutely nothing to do with what it says, and he just does the magical writing as a puppet of God?

Logic tells us that man was given a brain with which to think, just as he has eyes to see and ears to hear. History and logic tell us that there is no reason to think that Christ fulfilled the law against eating shellfish, or even touching pork.[xiii] Nor did his fulfilling the law take away the death penalty, nor the curse of women's uncleanness. So, the excuse that some of the fulfilled laws of the Old Testament are no longer necessary, but others are still in effect, does not really hold water. Man has chosen which ones to keep and which to sort of quietly ignore. As man has grown more experienced in his understanding of God, the actions and rules have changed and continue to change. The change is not a regression to sin; it is a progression to an understanding of what sin really is, what love really is, and what mankind really is. This change is a progression to truths about disease, mental illness, criminals, the church, hate, prejudice, and bigotry. With understanding come charity and a clearer recognition of God's will. He is the great I Am, not the great I Am Not.

Christians say we hate the sin and love the sinner, but if you go up to a wino on the street, a gay in a steam room, a thief in prison, or an adulterer in front of the church and ask them if they feel Christian love, do you know what they will say? Do you?

That is what we have made of Christ today in our efforts to prove we can make the people perfect, even though he couldn't! Instead of the one who loves the world, we have made him the one who hates the world.

Christians like Pat Robertson have blamed God for catastrophes that destroy people no more guilty than we are, but who live nearer the volcano.[xiv] Christians blame God for disease that terrorizes the world and praise him for destroying these sexual sinners with AIDS, and their children, and their wives, and their unborn babies.

We raise our voices in prayer and condemnation against other religions when we could be raising them to destroy poverty and disease. The earth could provide for its whole population if we worked toward that, but we do not make that happen; we fight over who owns the land. We are all guilty. I have two houses, while the majority in the world have none or have cardboard sheds. I have two coats while my brother goes cold. I have food that spoils while my sisters go hungry. I am well while my mother is sick. But Jesus proved we cannot do it alone. Our "greater work than he has done" requires a united voice of giving love, not condemnation of what our belief perceives as immorality.[xv] "The greatest of these is love" has a wider meaning than we really understand.

Let us spend our time in helping, caring for, and loving our brothers in sin, not feeling we must make them clean up before they come into our august presence. God is capable still of speaking to them in a still, small voice to worship him, in all the ramifications of the word *worship*, whenever he wants.[xvi] We are his hands to help, not his hands to destroy. We are speakers of the Word that brings life, not death. We are the bearers of hearts that bleed, not hearts that hate and condemn. God can do that if he wishes; we have another job to do. I fear, though, that we are not doing it very well.

One of the "great" Christians during WWII visited Adolf Hitler in Germany. When asked what Hitler looked like when he returned to England and his home church, he responded, "Hitler looked like Jesus, just as every other man does."

I cannot picture Jesus participating in the stoning of the woman or man caught in adultery, even if he or she had been caught doing it before. Can you? Perhaps some people can. I bet they would see tears in his eyes as he picked up the perfect rocks that would scrape and tear the sinner's flesh as his or her skull was crushed, too.

I'm sorry, my friend. That is not at all the way I see Jesus, or the Father, or the mother (Sophia). I don't think you do, either, nor does even Pat Robertson. Instead, we have all been blinded by the deceit of that which we could call Satan for the sake of simplicity. It is what makes us concentrate on the simplest of sins, like swearing or drinking, and overlook the substance, the reality of sin itself, like our willingness to let our brothers starve or to destroy a life because the person was born gay. We then allow real sin to survive and prosper under the cover of false righteousness—fighting silly battles like focusing on the protection of that supposedly great institution of marriage between one man and one woman (at least one at a time) instead of feeding the hungry or providing for the homeless and mentally ill.

Sin survives even in the guise of protecting "sacred" land, buildings, chairs, and symbols while turning aside the wounded and bleeding souls who might wander closer to the salt of the earth and receive some savoring. After all, they are not really our type of people, are they?

The recent turmoil about using an altar cloth that has lines from the Upanishads in a Christian church, or Buddhist statues placed in a Christian churchyard on days that celebrate religious unity, or allowing the church building to be used by different, non-Christian faiths on off days, reminds me of the turmoil in the church over the gay issue.

One dissenting (conservative) bishop in England said he couldn't support the Anglican hierarchy anymore partly because the archbishop is appointed by a secular government, but he felt it was totally righteous to invite over a bishop from South Africa to ordain deacons and so forth in his parish—even though it was in direct opposition to the covenants reached in the governing body of the church, not in the secular government. Further, while this South African bishop was opposed to gay marriage and gays in the priesthood, he had been a supporter of apartheid in South Africa. Now which "evil" is worse: allowing two people who love each other and want to commit publicly to each other to marry, or supporting the ultimate discrimination and racial bigotry of apartheid?

Eli: Again, would it be okay for the Assemblies of God to make bishops or presbyters—male or female—of a person who is sexually active with those the Bible condemns? Would it be okay with you? How about if he were sexually active with two women at once ... three ... a hundred ... or his sister, even?

Jay: Actually, I am certain the church has done that, though without knowing it, maybe. As far as being all right ... well, God did use an ass to speak for him, too.[xvii] I would say that these are all individual questions, and I cannot make a blanket statement on them.

The fact is, though, that the election of the openly gay and partnered Episcopal bishop caused a row not only in the American Episcopal Church, but in the Anglican as well.[xviii] Archbishop Rowan Williams, enthroned at Canterbury, is being pulled and pushed from the liberal side in the Northern Hemisphere and the ultraconservative side in the Southern Hemisphere.

Eli: I think it would be a stroke of genius for Rowan Williams to refuse to listen to the dog pack snapping at his heels—totally ignore them and do what is right, knowing he will stand before the great white throne of Jesus and give answer to all he has done in this flesh.

Jay: I, too, sometimes see the African bishops and the few conservative American leaders as a pack of dogs biting at Rowan's heels, and I agree that he does take them too much into account against his better judgment in a futile effort to hold the church together. But, eventually, he will see the spirit of wisdom and love moving in a new way and do what he knows is right for those who have been tortured, excluded, and put to death by biblical literalists and Koran memorizers. I am not sure that this understanding will occur until education is universal and thinking is not a sin, though.

Eli: That isn't precisely the way I meant that, as you know. Anyway, I pray Rowan's name is in the book of life. That would be a good thing.

Jay: Even though I do get frustrated with Rowan Williams's backsliding from his support of, and friendship with, homosexual clergy, I try to understand his perspective of the larger church and his reluctance to preside over the schism that is coming. Still, I believe he has the spirit, intelligence, and communicative ability to relate the truth when he finally succumbs to that truth. He will also then be able to espouse his acceptance to the world. Further, since Jesus came into the world not to condemn, and through him the whole world is saved, I would have to say that Williams's name is in the book of life.

Men and Political Correctness

Eli: I have heard it said that men need to be more masculine and stop trying to be politically correct all the time. Men are losing their roles in society. The differences in the sexes are dimming. The Bible indicates there is a place for men, and that is at the head of the family. Now, the politically correct club is trying to change even the words, the pronouns, in the Bible—like changing some occurrences of the word "he" to "she." That makes it more acceptable to enlightened folk; they act as if there is no difference between men and women. I have suspicions that some churches have female priests just to be politically correct in the eyes of the world. Others have suggested that female priests are there to make the church more attractive to men, because women are more nurturing and are mother figures. That is supposed to appeal to men. What is your take on that?

Jay: I doubt very much that the church allowed women to be priests to establish a mothering and nurturing image to draw in the men. I am sure they did this for equality. Women are just as capable of being priests as men are.

Eli: I remember the old truth: if you want your church to grow, if you want the family to be stable, get the men. Without them, the family is in jeopardy, and the church is, too. So, the point to me is the importance of the father in the family. I think we need to increase the worth and significance of the maligned men in society. This society, the creation of God, has a significant place for the manly man and the womanly woman—no mixing here. Each is determinedly needed. God, in the creation, made it so.

Jay: I thought you were for women, or whoever had a calling, being ministers? Now you seem to be saying they should be "womanly," and that indicates to me you want them to be in the home. Similarly, for a while, we argued from the assumption that you recognized homosexuality as being born and not chosen, and then you appeared to switch on me. Is this another switch? It's difficult to hit a moving target, you know.

Eli: I don't recall the switch. How did that happen? Did I misspeak or what? Like you said, the Bible says what it says. I didn't write it, so, like gravity, I can believe in it or not. That is my choice. At this time, I don't like the idea of jumping out of an airplane without a working parachute. So, I believe the Bible as it appears and do not try to be politically correct.

Jay: That is an interesting use of a gravity metaphor, putting it in an apples-to-oranges, logical fallacy. We have not agreed at all that the Bible is a natural law like gravity. Likewise, gravity does not lend itself to interpretation, while the Bible requires it—though you have not agreed to the interpretation part yet. As a side note, since gravity is the fundamental power in the universe, it is possibly the nearest force to God we can physically observe. As such, you might be able to actually create a logical comparison using the two, but it would require you to manipulate ideas for a long while. It could be fun, though.

But back to the real point: I was not aware that the being "politically correct" was a put-down on men or the man in the family. I see political correctness as an attempt to be sensitive to others, though it tends to get a bit ridiculous sometimes.

Times change; roles change; now it is difficult to keep women barefoot and pregnant in the kitchen. I recall my fundamentalist pastor's wife many years ago putting a sign on the door at her home that said "No Smokers or Women in Pants Allowed." And I distinctly recall the preachers saying a woman should not wear makeup, or she would be a Jezebel. Now, with the world smaller, we know that women in pants are not inherently evil, and the preacher's wife even sells makeup.

We do grow and change, don't we? And many of the changes are important and not just silly. I do not know the problem you refer to as the "role of men" being ignored or disappearing. I have never felt put down like that. Instead, I think the role of men is expanding and encompassing more of an intimacy with the family, perhaps because of the women's role expanding out of the home to the wider world.

Coincidentally, I am supposed to be writing a piece on the family for a magazine this month, an article titled "Love Makes a Family." It will be interviews throughout the state with families, especially families with gay parents, whether married, single, closeted, or out. As you probably know, after battling gay marriage, the next crusade of the far right is to stop gays from being able to adopt, even though statistics show that there is no inherent harm in it. Even the medical and psychological associations support it; but those endorsements just represent facts and statistics, which rarely figure in emotional or belief issues.

Now, let's look at your joke about your choosing to believe in the Bible being like your choosing to believe in gravity. I was just picturing someone saying he didn't believe in gravity and then floating away. It wouldn't happen; gravity is not a choice. One does not choose to be gay, either. It is not a choice, and increasingly people even outside of the medical and scientific realms are realizing this.

It does bring up the question, "What is choice?" Do we choose to get a cold, or to be smart or dumb? Do we choose to live in a democracy or an Islamic theocracy? Do we choose to be a man or a woman? Some choices are not really choices.

I was watching a program about Islam in the Indonesian area and how it is antithetical to the democratic system. One of the imams was saying that an Islamic state simply could not be a democratic state, as Indonesia is trying to be. If it were democratic, it would depend on what the people think of the laws of the land. An Islamic state would not care what the people think or how they vote; it is what Allah thinks and what is in the Koran that is the law. The people do not have to vote on anything.

I had to compare that to what the Christian literalists must believe—that the Bible has all the answers and rules—so we really would not need democracy for our nation either, would we? If God said it in the Bible, it would simply be the law, and since God said every word in the Bible, it would be a simple form of government. Of course, then the Senate and House could argue about various reasons why some rules are to be obeyed and others not, like your shellfish example, which you implied was God just making fun of the rule makers. I don't recall where he said that it wasn't really a law.

What would this Christian theocracy do with criminals who asked for forgiveness when we are supposed to forgive our brothers seven times seventy times a day? It doesn't work to say, "Well, we can forgive him, but he still has to pay the penalty." Isn't that what being forgiven means—not having to pay the penalty? Don't Christians believe Christ died to forgive our sins so we would not have to pay the penalty? If one still has to pay the penalty, is it still forgiveness? Or is this one of the situations for which purgatory was invented? One pays the penalty but only long enough to meet the crime, and then one is truly forgiven.

The way we perceive the world is what makes the world we see. I see the radical Christian as out to get gays. I see them as zealots incapable of understanding a being different from them. You see the liberal Christians as humanity denying the truth of the Bible, or at least watering it down through scientific or academic interpretations. Thus, the liberals seem to ignore the tenets of being transformed in the image of Christ.

The liberals see the image of Christ as reflecting the God of truth; thus, science and academia would only lead to more knowledge of him. The liberals see the Bible as a book of truths, perhaps mystically inspired by God, but filtered through the time and context of the many writers. Thus, like the Constitution, we must interpret it as scientific discoveries trigger new questions.

As the ability to transform the very DNA structure becomes a reality, we must now grapple with our understanding of life itself. As we begin to see what we assume to be the farthest reaches of the universe, we are in awe of the seeming miraculous natural laws, any one of which would, if changed by even an iota, negate the ability of the universe to support life. This presents us with challenges unforeseen by the writers of the Bible. Inevitably there will be questions. The answers will lead to new interpretations of the early writers who perceived the universe so differently from the way we do today.

Eli: I see the world and universe the way the Bible says they were created. The theories of space and time are changed all the time. People are trying to change the United States from what it was originally. Some are trying now to take "under God" out of the Pledge of Allegiance. There is a letter going around the Internet waking people up to this.

It is said that 86 percent of Americans believe in God. Therefore, I have a very hard time understanding why there is such a problem with having "In God We Trust" on our money and having "God" in the Pledge of Allegiance. Why don't we just tell the 14 percent to shut up and be quiet?

Jay: Oh, for goodness' sake! This sounds as bad as people crying, "My country, right or wrong! Love it or leave it"—absolute blarney! I realize this is not exactly what you were pointing to, but bear with me for a moment, and I will get to it.

"My child, right or wrong!" "My company, right or wrong!" If you really felt that your child was wrong, would you just ignore him and let him be wrong? Is it not your responsibility to correct him? If you love him, you will correct him. If you love your country, you will accept your responsibility to keep it on the right track. It is (or was) a government of, by, and for the people, wasn't it? If the people do not step up and say something is wrong, who will? Is that what the Germans said? Is that what the Russians said? Is that what Jefferson and Washington and Franklin and Paine said?

Besides, the pledge didn't have "under God" in it until the 1950s. Is that when we became Christian or Muslim? What were we for the two centuries before? As far as the majority ruling ... well, that is true, yes. But it is for the protection of the minority that the laws have to be set up. It was our protection of the weaker that freed the slaves and granted rights to women. It is to protect the children that we have laws, as they do not have a voice. The percentage of Americans who believe in a god has nothing to do with the constitutional issues involved here; such a suggestion is preposterous. As far as the 86 percent claimed in the letter goes, it might be good to examine which god a good portion of them believe in.

Gay Pride

The following dialogue refers to an article that tells of straight firefighters being required to participate in a gay pride parade in San Diego, California, in 2007. The gay participants and activists watching the parade shouted and made obscene gestures at the firefighters inside the fire truck when the firemen ignored them.[xix]

Jay: I couldn't say for sure if or how this harassment happened from just reading this partial story, so I looked up your source, and your Christian internet source had hundreds of interesting stories (one was that soy makes people gay!), so I tried to find a more reputable source covering the parade. I finally did find other references (though, from my personal experience, I do not doubt the parade happened; it happens every year).

The participants are much like the participants in the Mardi Gras parades in New Orleans and Carnival in Brazil. Odd—people celebrate the beginning of Lent with sexual promiscuity and overindulgence in food and drink, so not only gays are licentious in parades. Nevertheless, I agree these parades are many times grotesque—the pride parades and the Mardi Gras parades and many others. My comment is that the city was wrong. Forcing anyone to attend, firemen or school kids, is verboten in my opinion.

Now, the question, "of what is gay pride proud?" This is a bit complex, and I do not say it is the opinion of anyone but me. Let us look at the fundamentalist Christian as an example. When the world starts teaching evolution and taking the "under God" out of the pledge (which has been there since Eisenhower), and when Christians are spit on and mocked, they get upset. Their pride may be what is hurt.

Eli: That is true, sure. So, who thinks soy makes people homosexual? I have never heard of such, though there are many theories I have not encountered.

Jay: Well, it could be stereotyping, but when angry people accuse Christians of being bigots and closed-minded, the Christians often react by saying they are proud to be bigots.

Eli: That is only after they learn not to be fearful of the freeze words used to make them shut up and sit down—after they learn that both the accuser and accused are both bigoted, biased, prejudiced … and the list goes on.

Jay: I am not sure I would accept your argument there. You are just saying, "Everyone does it, and therefore it is okay," and that is not a good argument. But the original point was this: the gays for centuries have been spit on, beaten up, outlawed, murdered, and hated. When Stonewall happened—

Eli: What is Stonewall? Like Stonewall Jackson? I think I need some education here.

Jay: Very briefly, Stonewall refers to an incident that occurred in New York City wherein the gays fought back against the police who had been harassing and accosting them in a gay nightclub.[xx] It could be called the beginning of a rebellion—as the "proud to be a bigot" response is your reaction to a fundamentalist Christian being called a bigot. Is pride an overreaction to being liberated and out instead of being hidden and ashamed of being who they are?

I do not condone violence, and I do not think it is productive to what I believe God is doing, but I do understand what motivates it. Unfortunately, there is much in the gay community that is out of control, just as there is much in the straight community. Likewise, I am not able to judge too harshly those who fight battles I have not had to fight, like sadism-masochism or exhibitionism.

This is the crux: Since many Christians and people like the so-called Reverend Phelps ostracize the gays and tell them they are abominations and damned already, they have not found any reason to control their appetites. Plus, no code of conduct applies to them if they are not accepted as God's creations at the outset. Many of them know they fought the battle to be normal or straight most all of their lives, and their orientation could not change, so they had to accept that the fundamentalist Christian must be wrong, and that gays were therefore born gay. If the Christians were wrong about that, and the Bible was wrong about that, and the Bible is supposedly inerrant, something doesn't add up. So, what faith can they put in Christians who tell them they are not what they most certainly are (gay), and they are just being sinners and must quit it? What faith can they put in a Bible that tells them they are abominations and that the deity finds them abominations—or, more bizarrely, that God made them gay as a punishment for not worshipping him correctly (as it does in chapter 1 of Paul's letter to the Romans) and condemns them to hell for choosing to be abominations, while they know they didn't choose it? What part of the Bible should they believe?

Eli: That is an interesting thought. I will spend some time thinking about this. Another question: If gay pride is okay, and all beliefs are equal, why isn't anti-gay pride okay?

Jay: I actually do not have much to say about "gay pride" other than, and again only my opinion, it is a reaction to the world telling gays they are not acceptable human beings. It is an overreaction in many cases, and does not really help the cause often, but I understand why they do it. It's the old saying, "I'm mad as hell and I'm not going to take it anymore!" in action.

The basic premise of your anti-gay pride argument bothers me a bit, though. The two sides do not appear to be equal—or parallel, as the logicians say. It compares apples and oranges. For example, consider this statement made of the Vietnam debate (remember the sixties?): "If you are old enough to fight and die for your country, you should be old enough to drink legally in your country."

This sounds fair, sort of, but really, the two things are not parallel. The youth, strength, and malleability necessary to be a successful soldier are not the same qualifications needed to drink responsibly. Drinking requires a level of maturity notably lacking in youth. Further, there exists the possibility that the mature soldier might be more apt to question an order to "Take this hill!" than the youthful soldier.

Regarding your pride question, then, we have on one side a gay person who is saying, "I am proud of who I am and the way God made me." On the other side, we have a person not professing pride in himself, but simply proud of being against another person or, more likely, judging another person. A more balanced syllogism would be something along this line: if being pro-gay is okay, being pro-straight is okay. And it is. Compare this to "if being pro-gay is okay, being anti-gay is okay." It is not quite the same. Is it okay to be against someone being proud of who they are?

There is also a second level argument, and it rests on the term *okay*. We need to understand what your concept of "okay" is. Does the word reflect a moral judgment meaning "good"? Or does it mean fair or equal—more of "turnabout is fair play"? If it is only fair and equal, the term *okay* gains a little more credence in your "anti-gay pride" statement. If it means "acceptable morally," then we have to consider what, or whose, morality we are using as the yardstick.

As for it being *okay* to be proud of being gay, in either sense—meaning "good morally" or meaning "just and fair"—shouldn't one be happy or proud of who he or she is? I'm not saying what a person may *do*—just who he is. It is evident you believe being gay is not a state of being, but rather a choice, and definitely nothing to be proud of. You continue to feel free to ignore the scientists, psychologists, humanists, and students of history—and, even more strangely, a personal and present witness who lives it. You and many other Christians believe that one only has to look at a handful of biblical verses to say being gay is an abomination, wrong, and sin—and one does not have to think at all.

Consider another syllogism: if it is okay to have bigot pride, is it okay to have anti-bigot pride? Sometimes just plain common sense negates the need for confusion. So, no, I do not think it is okay to be anti-gay or have anti-gay pride.

BIBLIOLATRY

The writing discussed here is a sermon on substituting the Bible for God. The thesis of the sermon is the charge that there is an impediment or a boulder of bibliolatry holding some back from new visions and truths. That impediment is assuming the *Word of God* to be a mere book, the Bible.[xxi]

Eli: I don't know of anyone who worships the book. Do you? All I know love the Lord and honor, respect, and believe the text as inspired by him. So, the notion that the Bible is God is not called for, allowed, respected, or counted as believable by me in the presentation.

Jay: Interesting! This is the way many liberals perceive fundamentalists—as holding the Bible in too high of esteem, as inerrant and as more important than any factual science. If liberals are in error, and we could help them to see this, it could lead to better understanding.

I do not think liberals see bibliolatry as a worship of or a bowing down to a book on the altar. I think it is seen as unwillingness to read the book in a larger context than just the letter of the law. Liberals tend to lean to the spirit of the law. Why is it the law? What is to be accomplished by obeying this law? Does this law conform to the revelation of God's nature as revealed in all of his book and not just in this section, or in all of nature, or to all knowledge and understanding?

Eli: Now, in the scripture, my view is that Romans 12 admonishes us not to be conformed to the world but to be transformed by the renewing of the mind, bringing our mind into alignment with the revelation, prophetic word, and declarations of Christ, his apostles, and prophets, and the inspired Word of God as defined in the scripture.

Where today's prophets[2] speak in agreement with this Bible, this revealed Word of God, the church should 1) Listen; 2) Judge, measure, and compare the prophecy to the revealed word or scripture for believability; 3) Give the new prophecy time to reveal whether it is true, in the instances where it is not quite that believable (Psalms 105:18 and 105:19 mentions waiting for the word or promises to come to fruition." … till the time came …"); and 4) We look to the confirmation of two or three witnesses who are separate and not in contact with each other to see if God is making a statement that is verifiable over a large area of geography or population (2 Corinthians 13:1). We use other proofs, but this is enough for this discussion.

---

2   Eli's church and many other Pentecostal types of denominations often experience a congregant speaking aloud during the church service when "moved by the Spirit" and given a message, believed to be from God, to share. This message often includes a prophecy of the future or instructions to the church (or even to individual members). At times, this message is in the native language and understood by everyone; at other times, the speaker speaks in an unknown tongue, and another congregant must interpret aloud for the rest of the people present what God has said through the unknown tongue. The Pentecostals see these as demonstrations of "the gifts of the spirit" spoken of in chapter 12 of 1 Corinthians. The idea of continuing revelation directly from God is found in varying forms in many other denominations as well. The Latter-Day Saints, or the Mormons, title the president of the denomination a prophet, and he ostensibly receives updates from God. For example, in the mid-twentieth century the president of the church said God now wished to allow the priesthood to be bestowed on African American men, who had until then been denied access to that most fundamental of titles in the LDS denomination.

We do not worship the scripture. We hold it as wise, true, trustworthy, and practical in our daily lives.

When one comes out and says that God has given him a revelation that is not in keeping with the clear word of God, we ask for scripture, confirmation, and time to see the results of that lifestyle, doctrine, or teaching.

I believe homosexuality, stealing, drunkenness, brothel attendance, and such activities to be of the world, not of the character and lifestyle of Christ. The key is Christ. Does he practice, approve of, and praise such things? Or does he say they are not part of his creation and purpose? He clearly says stealing is out. Adultery is out. Coveting is out, when it is focused toward what your brother or neighbor possesses. If it is focused toward the gifts of the Holy Spirit, then, coveting is good and to be done, for his apostle said to the Corinthians to covet earnestly the best gifts.

Jay: In my thinking, when a person extrapolates a doctrine from a part of the scripture that the Bible does not teach throughout the book, as a whole, it is not reliable and often leads to a teaching that is not in the revealed character of Christ.

The Tower of Babel story is a good example of the larger principle in the story overriding the incidentals of the tale.[xxii] God multiplied the languages of man to stop man from completing a city and a tower to reach into heaven. The gods (plural there) state that if man were allowed to continue as he was, and he continued to progress and reach his full potential, there would be nothing man could not do. So, the gods created multiple languages and threw the workers into confusion. Well, we can trace the languages of the world even now to their root languages. Linguists also understand pretty well how languages change and evolve from one to another. It is very doubtful that the division of languages occurred in the twinkling of an eye. So, I see the point of the story of Babel more along the line of pride not being acceptable (in this case, trying to be like God).

53

The examination of the story does not seem to agree with other hints at God's nature. God's stated purpose—let us stop them by confusing their languages, because if we do not confuse their languages, there is nothing they cannot do—doesn't correspond to "be ye perfect," does it? I would argue that perfection is a reaching of full potential.

If we take this story literally, as you prefer, there are several difficulties for me. I do not see multiplying the language that all men spoke (and what language was it, anyway?) to have been intended to stop people from building a rock tower. Besides there being a natural limit to how tall a tower can be, the workforce does not need to communicate in one language even today. Unskilled workers who do not speak English do much of the manual labor in the United States, for example. And the language of engineering is more math and drawings. So, to stop the building of a tower, changing languages instantaneously seems like a waste of a perfectly good miracle. Why not just huff and puff and blow the tower down? So, I consider taking the story literally to be an error.

It is not a matter of whether a god *could* instantly infuse thousands of people with myriad languages, each a distant relation to another. Sure. Would it be logical for the actual, stated reason (stopping the building)? Not really. Would it be a great story to demonstrate through myth how languages might have come into being to a people who did not have opportunity to understand the geographic multiplicity of language development? Yes, perfectly. Again, I have to say that much of the Bible is not meant to be taken literally. We are to use our minds, not just our eyes.

Eli: My take on the Babylon story is this: God told mankind to populate the entire earth. Man, Nimrod, the king of Babylon, determined to take things another direction. He said, "Let me be the only one who hears God, and all of you people do as I say." Maybe that is the first idea of a pope.

God said, "I want a million guys listening to me," so he gave a million languages, or derivatives thereof, or dialects and such, to set the peoples on the road to filling all the earth. It's simple to me. It appears God does not need a super government, or nationality, or church, in order to joyfully answer the prayers of all who are living in his grace and joy of life.

The people's ability to accomplish anything to which they put their resources of speech, having one goal and one purpose to accomplish the goal, is a statement of how powerful the Lord created them. They have a creative ability—a finite expression of the infinite God in whose image they were originally made.

Jay: For one who takes the Bible literally, this interpretation seems to stretch the story of Babylon beyond literalism. The statement made by God is that the gods must stop them, or men will be able to do anything they set their minds to. Are you taking a literal story and applying a metaphorical meaning to it, then? It seems so. Two points: God stops the building of a city and tower, but the city and other cities get built. This miracle didn't stop man from achieving. But the division of languages appears to be one fundamental cause, or at least a dominant contributor, to the eternal lack of peace in the world. The different nations and languages do not understand one another and yet must communicate. War often results from differing paradigms and philosophies. The language one speaks, and thus in which one thinks, fosters differing views of man, the world, even life.

Anyway, back to the original question: do people put the Bible on a pedestal and make it equivalent to God? Do you think the idea the sermon presents, then—that love for the scriptures is tainted when scripture, and not God, becomes the object of worship—applies to you?

Eli: Who does this? No one does in my circle.

Jay: Actually, you present to me many times the connection of Jesus and the text. The way I understood you, anyway, was that the Word is Jesus and Jesus is the Word, and the Word is the Bible and Jesus is the incarnate Bible. Did I misunderstand you?

Eli: Generally, that is correct. The parallel thought: You say things, use words to express thoughts and concepts, musings, speculations … the words are you … in a limited form.

Another form of God is the coming of the Spirit unto the Old Testament prophets. The Spirit gives inspired, breathed revelation, prophetic speech—called prophecy when spoken and scripture when written. Yet another expression of God is the Logos, the Word, becoming flesh in Jesus.

Jay: Rather than setting the Bible on an altar and bowing down before it, I think the meaning of bibliolatry here is more along the line of inerrancy and interpreting all of it literally. The Bible is so holy and perfect that it is like a god and cannot be less than correct.

Eli: I think you know what side I am on. I believe God is opinionated and can see through a keyhole with both eyes at once … in all of his compassion.

Jay: I do not think God is opinionated. Nor do I think he is a bigot. He does not form an opinion about what is right and wrong; he *exists* in the right. I suppose the only discussion that can continue on this relates to the Bible itself.

Is the Bible the only, unadulterated, correctly interpreted, physical presence of Christ on this earth? You think it is eternally true, and the men who wrote it and the time in which they lived did not have any influence in it. Therefore, referencing the six or so biblical statements in the entire Bible on the subject, you believe

God is the one who speaks against homosexuality. I say the biblical attitude toward people who are by nature homosexual is not what God intends, and the men who wrote from their own time and understanding of the world and of man created that attitude, not God. They perceived that to be the will of God based on their own understanding of their world and God. That appears to be our only point of argument.

If, as you hold, the Bible is absolutely and literally true, and is the *only* Word of God to the humans on earth, then your arguments are stout. Your arguments don't really answer several problematic biblical concepts, though. We do not, for example, strictly adhere to the Pauline statements in the second chapter of 1 Timothy speaking against women being in authority and in favor of women obeying their husbands, or the guidelines on who should or shouldn't wear head coverings in 1 Corinthians 11, or the admonitions regarding sex during menstruation in Leviticus chapter 20. Consider also the Old Testament writings in Leviticus 21 about the physically imperfect priests not being welcome to serve at the altar of God, and the morning and evening without the sun in the creation stories—but I suppose we can redefine sunrise and sunset without the sun, can't we? I mean, why bother with scientific or observable phenomena if we have God already totally defined by his Word, huh? It does not seem to me that the Bible is accepted by very many as the unblemished Word of God. It seems imperfect and even wrong in places.

I think Jesus said something about this Word when he talked about divorce, didn't he? Moses (*Moses*, not God) gave you this law of divorce because of the hardness of your hearts.[xxiii] This is *not* God's desire. But we learn this "Moses opinion" is the Word: inerrant, perfect, absolute, without needing any human interpretation of what is written there. In fact, didn't the Jews follow it for centuries as from God?

What the heck? We are taught this stuff in Sunday school as children. When we become adults, maybe we should look at this

Word a little more maturely, with adult minds that can reason better. Maybe we can reason together with the Word and see what it might really mean. Maybe the writers wrote to the best of their knowledge and ability, but we have more knowledge now. The sun doesn't orbit the earth and does not stop in the sky.

Think on this: the fundamental, human animal drive to reproduce is in the mythos of the Bible. The heterosexual reads that God made woman as a helpmate for man because, as God says, it is not good for man to be alone. There is recognition that man needs to love and be loved. This is great for the heterosexual. But gays, because they can only love the same sex romantically, are simply denied a helpmate to love, and that is not acceptable to what God says about man being alone. The gay person does not choose the inability to love the supposed opposite sex that way. So, does God simply ignore this part of his creation, his complete human race? Gay people must not need the same things that straight people need. This is not God; this is mankind's fear and hatred of "the other."

Eli: The straightforward answer to this is that the homosexual man is free to choose any woman to love, just as everyone else is, and the homosexual woman is free to love a man just as the straight person is.

Jay: No. Not so. The gay person is constitutionally not attracted to the opposite sex, just as you are unable to be attracted physically to me. It is this quality of loving the helpmate, being physically attracted to him or her, that makes the bond. If this helpmate bond did not have to be romantic and sexual, Adam could have loved another created man in the creation story. Then, we would indeed have Adam and Steve, as the fundamentalist taunt goes. But Adam was evidently not gay and required a woman to love. And, yes, I am aware of the command to fill the earth with your seed. I am merely demonstrating a related point.

Gays are able only to have romantic attraction to the same sex. Even though there are only two sexes when one looks at genitalia, ignoring the many cases of abnormal birth defects, the medical field is beginning to recognize that there are not just two, but numerous genders emotionally and mentally, and these genders do not always line up with the genitalia presented.

Very few people are totally straight, for example. I believe it was Kinsey who postulated that sexual orientation really exists on a scale—being somewhere between totally gay and being totally straight. Even most straight people are not totally straight. Sexual orientation is not as black-and-white as it is portrayed so often in life and in the Bible.

Why doesn't the Bible go into this complex sexuality? It doesn't need to; that is not its purpose. It also doesn't try to offer medical evaluations in its stories, though we would both grant that God knows about germs and disease and such. Instead we are told in the Bible that victims of disease and mental illness are either being punished by God or are possessed by the devil or demons. In one case, Jesus even tells us that this man has suffered being blind his whole life merely so God can demonstrate his power to heal.[xxiv] Oh, please! Why not just use one who was born blind already ... or were they all crippled to prove a point? And, if so, why doesn't he heal them, too? What kind of parent would do that to his child? Yet, we are to believe that the loving God created a cripple just to show his power? I don't buy it!

This loving God, we are told in the flood story, destroys all of mankind except Noah's immediate family.[xxv] Are the other babies evil sinners? Have they been stealing each other's diapers or lusting after the little girl in the next tent? Have they been blaspheming or swearing in gibberish? This flood narrative story conveniently echoes the Sumerian-Babylonian flood story wherein the gods destroy mankind because he is too noisy or something. The gods then repent of it and save one man and his wife. The gods give this man, Utnapishtim, and his wife eternal life and place them in a garden of jeweled flowers reminiscent of the jeweled city and the pearly gates that descend from heaven.[xxvi] Is this flood story really there to demonstrate a larger truth about immortality and death, or to purport that evil displeases the gods or God, or even to answer a real, local, major flood event that actually occurred in the far distant past? This is the job of myth.

Consider also the oft-referenced cities of Sodom and Gomorrah.[xxvii] Prior to the story of Lot and the angels, Abraham has been arguing with God, trying to get him to repent of the plan to destroy the evil cities on the plains. Finally, God promises not to incinerate them if only fifty, and then forty, and finally only ten righteous people are therein. Doesn't it seem reasonable that babies and children are people? Are they not even now referred to as innocent? And even babies in the womb, espoused by conservatives as being fully human, must have been present in these cities. Doesn't it then seem reasonable to assume there were ten righteous? Or do only men count? And how old do they have to be to count?

I don't mean to be picky, but the Bible, the Word, is not an automobile manual that tells how the machine works. It is philosophical. The automobile manual does not deal with the beauty or ugliness of the car, or offer eschatological reasons for the car's existence, but the Bible deals openly with this subjective portrait of man: Is man beautiful, good, and connected to his brother? Is he living and dying for a purpose, and what is that purpose?

The Bible does not entertain the question of how many calories or how many vitamins a day are required for man to work well. It doesn't tell us how to pull a tooth or take out a cancerous tumor. It does tell us that man is valuable, worth caring for. It tells us repeatedly that God loves man and that he expects man to be his brother's keeper.

To me, the Bible is the attempt by many men over many centuries to find answers to questions of existence. But the answers the men came up with are necessarily the product of what these various writers knew and understood. And this knowledge, influenced by their personal philosophies, exists in direct relation to humanity's given location on the chart of history and history's changing interpretation of the universe in which we live in the dimension of space-time.

Boycott for Christ

Jay: My editor just asked me to write a news story about a pool-cue company that is naming a cue after a gay-bashing episode of a television show.[xxviii] I'm not really sure how I should approach it: turn the other cheek (pardon the pun) or fight it. Should we boycott the company? Should it be a public, organized boycott like the Ford boycott by the Christian Right in opposition to Ford offering equal benefits to gay partners just as they do to straight partners?

Eli: First, I don't watch the series you refer to, by choice. What I have seen makes me think it should not exist. Now, that is a bigoted and biased opinion. I'm not ashamed of it. People who use others as cattle— animals to be fed upon as a dog eats a sheep—are not to be allowed by a society or a government. Thus, we can see the need for the city police, militia, and military of a nation.

Jay: I wouldn't argue that with you. But do you think I should call for a boycott of the pool-cue company, as you did against the Ford Company?

Eli: I think it a good approach to first appeal to the company or to him. Tell him of the offense he has caused, and give him a chance to comply with your sensitivities. (Bill Ford, on the other hand, said he would stay neutral. Some executives spoke with him. He reneged. He was told he was going to be boycotted. He continued to support financially the homosexual agenda.)

Second, if he continues to offend you, go higher, to the legalists, and see what the options are, and let him know from the attorney what your options are and what you plan to do about it. Then get on with your life. Let the ones among you who have sworn to fidelity do it. Let them all be good in the sight of Christ. Get on with being citizens who are a good example for all to see! Find a real way to bless him; tell him how to make money without insulting you and without promoting the indignity that the stick indicates.

We told Ford that if he stops aiding and abetting the homosexual agenda, we would quickly purchase Ford products. Until then, we were going to watch his sales slip into oblivion! It would have been easy to fix. Repent, Bill Ford!

Jay: Of course, Ford was supporting people, as opposed to seeming to endorse violence.

Eli: As we see it, Ford was endorsing the destruction of family norms, biblical norms, and Christian values.

Jay: And the pool-cue company is capitalizing on hate to make money, but … any thoughts? And if we did call for a boycott, would the same community support us against gay hate as supported the Christians against gay love?

Eli: I don't think it is a hate issue. It is a moneymaking issue. Some things sell on TV. As for support, years ago, I did go to war with the Carter administration and their Delphi Oracle, which gave their definition of a family. Fundamentalist Christians allied with the Mormons against this common enemy. Carter and associates were trying to redefine the family.

We knocked the Carter train off the tracks here. Christians and Mormons, together for a short time, got their wording synchronized. Carter's stooges went home with their tails between their legs. The next week, the Christians were taking on the Mormons again.

Though I am not for the cue sticks and their message, I am not even near endorsing the idea that the homosexual community and the beliefs expressed there are defendable. When we see a clear and consistent Christian belief system from them, and we hear statements that the character of Christ is the goal, that will be a step in the right direction.

Jay: I would have to ask, then, which character of Christ is the goal—the all-inclusive, the one who doesn't condemn, or the one who broke the law of the Sabbath and, when criticized for breaking God's law, said that the Sabbath was made for man, rather than man for the Sabbath?[xxix]

Eli: Hey, old friend … you are a crafty one, methinks. I am leaning toward the idea that I am correct, and those who disagree with me are intolerant and are exhibiting hate. What do you think?

Jay: I would not be at all surprised if many of those who disagree with you do exhibit hate and intolerance. I am sorry it has come to this; however, being intolerant of intolerance is not really the same thing as being intolerant of gay couples receiving equal treatment. The gays are not attacking your marriage rights; the fundamentalists are attacking the gays' right to marry the ones they love.

Look at the argument in this light: one group is seeking to deny a right; the other is simply seeking a right. Let's look at a different example. Many conservative Christians are very upset by the denial of prayer as part of a school activity, like at football games or graduation ceremonies. Most do not appreciate the concept of the separation of church and state. The liberals do not want prayer as a school-sanctioned activity. The conservatives see this as a denial of a basic right, and in a sense, it is. It is a denial of the conservative's right to bring one's own philosophy or religion unasked into the public arena. But this denial is not against the conservative or a person who wants to pray. He can pray, but he cannot infringe on the rights of those who do not wish to participate in that prayer. This becomes a constitutional question, really.

The gay-marriage right does not infringe on the rights of another person; it does contradict the conservative beliefs, though. That is true. But all Americans are entitled to their own beliefs; they simply cannot usurp the beliefs of, nor deny the rights of, others. Gay marriage does not take away any of the rights of the conservative; it only goes against his or her belief.

As a side note, I sometimes wonder if the fundamentalist Christian would be as adamant about allowing prayer in the public schools if the prayer were to Allah and practiced on prayer rugs, or to Krishna, or to the emperor. I rather expect the Christians envision a simple prayer in the tradition of begging their own God's blessing on whatever is happening. Of course, in Hinduism, there are many true gods, so to which god should they pray? I may be wrong about this, but I can almost hear the outrage now.

Eli: I think we ignore the rights of the Christian by denying him the right to pray.

Jay: He can pray anytime, anywhere. He cannot make others participate in that prayer—at least at a state-sponsored activity. And listening is participating. After all, at a church service, one prays while the congregation participates in silence or chimes in with a few amens.

GAY MARRIAGE

⁓

Eli: Matt Barber, an attorney with Concerned Women for America, has some strong opinions against gay marriage. He claims that homosexuals have a lobby and are supported by the "leftist press," and that this lobby has invented the terms "marriage equality" and "gay rights," and the terms are dishonest attempts to sway opinion by comparing gay issues to the civil-rights fights of the 1960s.[xxx]

Jay: Well, marriage equality means receiving the social, tax, and other advantages equally, so what would it be called? Gay rights, let's see: the right to be free from physical and verbal attacks; the right to visit your loved one in the hospital and not be turned away because you are not family; and so on. These are rights and are just drops in the bucket in the overall equality imbalance. I think trying to argue the just use of the terms "equality" and "rights" is simply a straw-man fallacy thrown into the debate. As an attorney, Barber should know this very well.

I just wrote a story on a young man whom the authorities kicked out of the United States Coast Guard for being gay. He told an executive officer, as part of a mission-security report, about an attempt to blackmail him because he was gay. He "told" in order to protect the ship he was on and the anti-smuggling activities the

Coast Guard was pursuing. He was a good serviceman and didn't do anything in port that a good many heterosexual sailors do all the time. Why was he singled out for discharge? It was only because he had hooked up with a man and not a woman, like the other sailors. This doesn't seem to be equal treatment. Intriguingly, the lesbians on the ship were never bothered. Could it be because two women together is sort of a men's fantasy for some reason?

Eli: I can't say why the lesbians were not kicked out. They should have been. It would be equal treatment.

Jay: You allow equal punishment, but not equal rights. Interesting.

Eli: Barber also claims gays want a secular humanist society where everyone has to not just accept, but "celebrate high-risk, unnatural and fruitless homosexual behaviors," that gays want a society without differences in the sexes—a sexual androgyny—and morals that are relative instead of God's expressed absolute. Do you agree with that?

Jay: Why on earth would any intelligent gay person give a bat's wing whether some straight guys and gals celebrated their having sex? As to the "high-risk, unnatural, and fruitless," adjectives—well, let's start with "fruitless": how many married couples use birth control, whether in the form of pill or prayer? I am not sure what he means by "high-risk." Many gay practices are also present in heterosexual couples as well. I would agree that gays have more sexual encounters than many straights, though I see some complex causes there. "Natural" … well, what is natural? Is masturbation natural? Is the missionary position the only natural position?

What is very natural for heterosexuals doesn't necessarily seem at all natural to homosexuals. Now, I am *not* talking about sex with animals or relatives or chairs. Again, those are not actions for me to argue; I do not find myself attracted to them and would be speaking outside my understanding. God will have someone else who can speak for those children of his.

As far as blatantly differentiating the sexes versus endorsing androgyny, one does not change inherent distinctions; they are inherent. As for androgyny, many gays would turn their noses up at an androgynous male or female. I hear gay men say all the time, "If I wanted a woman, I would get a woman." Those men do not seek androgynous people (though there are some who do). There are also cross-dressers and drag queens, but many of them are straight. That is, again, a different area and not mine to argue.

Eli: He also claims that homosexuals don't really want marriage at all. They are just using it as a tool to destroy the institution of marriage itself and to make homosexual behavior a norm.

Jay: They seek marriage because they don't want marriage? Bull! Does one join the Communist Party to destroy it? Does one become a Christian to destroy Christianity?

Eli: Again, he says that "marriage equality" is a false description of what the gays desire. Everyone in the United States can marry. But marriage is to remain as a vow between a man and a woman.

Jay: And, again, his reasoning makes one's head spin. The very definition of marriage as being between one man and one woman is exactly what gays seek to change. I am also angered at this ridiculous argument that if we let gays marry, then why not allow people to molest children and marry their mothers and have weddings where we kill the bride and the whole marriage party has sex with her dead body.

Gays are gays; they do not want to marry anyone in their close family any more than straight people want to. *Please,* do not ever use that argument or the protest against bestiality with me. I find it personally offensive and totally off the subject. I am dealing with a real situation here. It is *not* a mental illness; it is a biological fact.

The question is how to rectify the mistaken images of this biological fact—especially when otherwise decent people assume that writers hundreds or even thousands of years ago knew all about human sexuality when they appeared to condemn some of its biological forms. Likewise, carefully consider the biblical admonitions as to whether they were referring to real homosexuals or to sex vendors and slaves. Both types of homosexual activity are part of the Bible.

And, as far as Barber's concept that gay marriage is a cover for the takeover of secular humanism … I hardly know what to say of that paranoia. Most gays, even the intelligent ones, could not even tell you what secular humanism is. Nor would they care. You say this guy is an attorney; I wonder if he may have skipped logic classes.

There, you have my comments. Are there any intelligent arguments against gays we can deal with?

BIGOTRY

Eli: *As far as bigotry goes, I think it is fair to say the writers of the pro-homosexual persuasion are in fact bigoted, biased, and prejudiced. The bigots in the news media and at the universities have to face the fact that they are bigots, too! How do you respond to this? I think it is easy for the pot to call the kettle black ... looking at things from another set opinion. Back to Christ: how would he then live, think, and respond to humanity?*

Jay: As far as you seeing the press or the educational institutions, or even the liberals, as bigoted, biased, and prejudiced, or the kettle being black as well: I have to disagree. Is fighting against hate crimes prejudice? Is putting statistics out on the percentage who have no fears about allowing gay marriage or domestic partners bigoted?

There is a definite bias in much of the press and in the universities—at least those that allow alternative views to be debated and not just denied. I have no problem with their being biased; everyone who has an opinion is biased. So is the news. We only need to know the bias, and we can read the biased article with that knowledge and still get something from it. I even get things from the Fox News team, but I am totally cognizant of their bias.

As to how would Christ respond ... well, how did he respond? He accepted everyone from tax collectors to centurions and whores, though he did condemn the churchmen. He also bad-mouthed the Samaritans and the non-Jews. As far as the gays, he undoubtedly was aware of their existence in the Roman society, at least. He never seemed to say anything about it himself. He did not condemn those born blind or crippled or epileptic. I doubt very much he would condemn those born gay, either. And again, there is a difference between the homosexual relations going on in the Greek and Roman societies and the people who are truly homosexual and not just seeking physical pleasure and variety.

Jesus would encourage gay people to love one another, and he would encourage a sincere and probably monogamous relationship (unlike our conservatives today, who disallow the marriage or union of two people and the rules that could follow.) The saying that these people can't marry because they are not understood leads inexorably to promiscuity. If we aren't supposed to be together in a loving relationship, why bother following the rules of the people who supposedly do belong in a monogamous relationship?

You told me you were a bigot. Actually, you bragged that you were a bigot. A bigot is one who discounts any contrary evidence to a preconceived belief, isn't it? I'm sorry, but I do not think that is a praiseworthy position. What if Joseph had been bigoted about his fiancé's pregnancy? Or consider what happened to Pharaoh when God presented him with all sorts of "facts" that he could see with his own eyes, but chose to ignore.

Eli: What of the bigot who thinks his position is a new revelation when it is an old one in a new head? He desires that his so-called new position should hold sway over the "old" position. What of the unchanging wisdom of the eternal God who thinks he is right or correct at all times?

Remember Lucifer, who said he had a better way for creation to live, to think, and to act![3]

Who defines morality: the creator or the created? The battle comes down to the question of who the creator is. Is it the slow evolution of human sociological impulse, or was man created in the image of the divine and then slowly degraded by sinful or erroneous habits that evolved our initial perfect society into the present flawed one?

Jay: First, what society was perfect in the beginning? The Garden of Eden was sealed off from even the first man and woman—definitely not a perfect society. Noah survived the destruction of the entire earth, annihilated because it wasn't a perfect society. Even though these examples are mythic in nature, they indicate a constantly fallen world, as you would say. And the slow evolution of human social impulse brought about women's rights, the abolition of slavery, and the lie being put to the onetime Christian belief that slavery was God's intent. The slow evolution of society birthed democracy and monotheism and even Christianity. Why do you assume that this sociological growth is bad just because we are now recognizing that

---

3   I am not even going to try to present the multitude of opinions and references for the concept of Lucifer. However, what Eli is referring to here is the generally held belief of many fundamentalists that is taken from references in Ezekiel 28 and Isaiah 14. That belief is that Satan (or Lucifer, or the devil under any other name) was the most beautiful angel, and he allowed pride to lead him to challenge God's dominion. He decided he could govern better than God and gathered a third of the angels in heaven to his camp in war against God. God and his angels then cast Lucifer out of heaven, and he fell to earth, where he tempts mankind and awaits the final battle with God when the world comes to an end. The ambiguity of the Lucifer/Satan myth is fascinating and confusing. One of the stories even has Lucifer loving God so much he will bow only to God and not, as directed by God, to God's creation, man, and he thus is cast out of heaven for loving God too much, it seems. Milton's *Paradise Lost* contributes to the mythology, as do many similar myths in world religions. It is sufficient to say in this instance that to Eli, Lucifer is Satan and the number-one enemy of God and man. He was the serpent in the Garden of Eden and is/was the dragon in the book of Revelation.

human sexuality is not the simple process we pretended it was for millennia?

What did it take for Peter to give up his bigotry about letting non-Jews into the fold of Christianity? Just because we have based our own, worthless lives on a deep-seated belief does not, really and truly, make that deep-seated belief true.

That is a difficult fact. I know that in order for one to give up a deep-rooted belief upon which one has based one's entire existence, one must find a decent replacement. I am trying to offer one, but it has an awful lot of "salt" on it, so it takes a while. And, believe it or not, I am not asking you to leave behind righteousness or God. I am only saying there is even a more perfect way.

Eli: My laughing at the idea of bigotry is the same as my laughing at the politically correct take on tolerance. Who are the bigots? All who oppose us! Recently a Catholic man was fired from his job for stating his conviction, his belief, and his decision about the issue of homosexuality. He called it deviant behavior. The homosexual community wanted him fired for being insensitive and intolerant.

What a laugh! One-way tolerance! It is beyond being a joke; it is tyranny! It is time for what is politically correct to come down. Certainly God can forgive, love, and draw to him all kinds of people. No contest there. When one says God has made him to think and act in a manner that is decried from the beginning to the end of the scripture, now that is a real draw on the credible. When black is white and white is said to be black, that is a big reach.

Did you know some judges in Australia want to be free to practice pedophilia? They think it is a good thing, if the child consents. It is still against the law thus far; I wonder how much longer?

*So, are there any bigoted, prejudiced, or biased people in the crowd? I think they all are, as seen in the scope of "All have sinned and come short of the glory of God."*xxxi *So, I am just looking at the hypocrisy of* *the detractors, slinging mud that is supposed to make us be silent in the face of freeze words! Jesus is alive. The Bible is true. Jesus is truth. So it has been and will always be.*

Jay: First, *bigotry* and *intolerance* are not freeze words. They are nouns that indicate a particular activity or trait. The fact that you call them freeze words indicates that they carry some authority even to the fundamentalist mentality. Evidently, at one time, some Christians did not want to be bigots or intolerant—it seemed sort of anti-Christian in the past, perhaps.

Evidently you or a fellow bigot, as you proudly claim to be, at one point decided the best defense is a strong offense, so you started calling the critic of bigotry "bigoted." Well, it may sound good, but as I've stated before, bigotry is denying a *truth* to maintain a *belief* that may very well be untrue. Bigotry is not being faithful to a supposedly put-upon God. It is, for example, ignoring the truth to support a preconceived belief that a collection of ancient writings is magically perfect when absolutely nothing else in this world is. Being a bigot does not amount to simply disagreeing with something, as you seem to think.

If the first chapter of the Genesis account is supposed to be inerrant, I have some questions. There was evening and morning the first day, but God did not create the sun and moon (which were to give light and rule the day and night) until the fourth day. Yet, in the same chapter, evening and morning define a day. Now, excuse me, but if we want to be technically correct, days are defined by the rotation of the earth and the sun rising and setting.

Do we have to redefine words, or even language, as well as literature, to make this story true? And what, pray tell, is the water above the firmament (the sky) that is separated from the water beneath the firmament? I'm not going to buy that it is clouds, as there are heavens above the clouds, too; I've flown there, and so have you. Is this perhaps space, and it isn't a vacuum, but really water?

And was woman really an afterthought because Adam didn't have a helpmate, even though he did a pretty good job of naming every animal, vegetable, and mineral during the same day in which he was put to sleep and a woman was created from his rib? That is a damned fast naming of every species, all of which of course did not develop through evolution but were created fully formed.

I would accept these discrepancies as totally irrelevant if the stories were allowed to be mythic in nature: in other words, if they were stories that demonstrated a truth larger than the story itself—the truth that was to be taken from the story, rather than the story being true literally. But since you insist I have to take the story as inerrant and literal, I have a little trouble.

Eli: You are not sounding particularly tolerant. Try considering this in your thinking, a quote about a well-known Christian theologian and cultural leader:

> *Last week, Dr. Ted Baehr told the Inaugural Summit on Peace and Tolerance, a conference of international Christian, Muslim, Jewish, and political leaders, that tolerance is not the answer, but Jesus Christ and God's love is.*
>
> *"Tolerance is wrong," Dr. Baehr said. "I don't tolerate my kids staying up late. I don't tolerate my kids talking back. Man is always trying to establish a new global order. There is a global order, but the global order of Jesus Christ is the only true global order because it's based on love and truth, not tolerance.*
>
> *"The Bible says you have to be loving if you're from God. If you're not loving, you're not from God. But, God's love does not tolerate evil or falsehood."*[xxxii]

Can you accept his definition and examples of tolerance?

Jay: First, I am amazed that he allegedly evoked Jesus as the author of global order at a conference of Christian, Muslim, and Jewish participants, but I won't dwell on that. I assume he was an invited speaker and undoubtedly provided much conversation there. There are different kinds of tolerance, or perhaps I should say degrees of or motivations for tolerance. Again, his appears to be a simplistic argument starting out with a preconceived result. An argument offers proofs and listens to the other side(s) to find the truer. I say "truer" because many arguments are arguments for the simple reason that there is not an ultimate understanding of the situation available, and we have to do our best to find the answer. This gentleman attempts to destroy the concept of tolerance as positive. He assumes, I am guessing here, that since people call him intolerant or bigoted, he can escape that charge by trying to take the offense—making it a good thing to be too proud to look at evidence: "My mind is made up, so don't confuse me with the facts—and what's more, I will not tolerate your doing or believing anything that I, personally, have decided is not my way."

I'll bet he does tolerate walking in the rain, paying taxes, changing diapers, people starving if he doesn't have to see them, and myriads of other things he may not be happy with, but tolerates. So, is he really intolerant, or just opinionated or ignorant or stubborn? We can make all of these positives. I don't tolerate ignorance, or bigotry, or stupidity without at least grimacing; I would say that I am definitely intolerant of those things.

Not tolerating kids staying up late or talking back is okay, but one needs to look at the whole premise. Some parents do not find anything wrong or inherently evil or un-Christian about kids staying up late. Actually, the human teen operates better on a late night and late morning schedule just for health and clarity of his thought. Talking back has its own levels, but its regulation is a personal choice within the family.

Some parents do not even have a problem with kids talking back because they do not demean the child. Instead, they attempt to teach the child to make intelligent choices through reasoning. If a kid talks back in anger, we can hit them; violence clarifies a lot of gray areas in the realm of good and bad, doesn't it? Of course, they cannot hit us in return, or we can have them stoned—and this biblical injunction does not refer to marijuana.

Additionally, the article you cite does not depict a parent exercising his responsibility to teach a child to survive in the world. The instruction that is to be taken from Baehr is not regarding how one should raise the young to help them survive.

Instead, his argument is to encourage the Christian fundamentalist to not tolerate, or put up with, or allow, any philosophy, or religion, or truth, or interpretation, but that which he espouses. I doubt he would encourage Islamic intolerance, though. His argument is not about children; it is a non-toleration of anyone else's way of thinking.

I am sure, with your travels, you can see what not tolerating those who refuse to accept a one and only truth is like in Indonesia, and Pakistan, and Afghanistan. Bin Laden does not tolerate those who do not accept his truth. Bin Laden would probably not tolerate his children talking back to him either.

Toleration is a good word. It has a positive meaning as well as Baehr's negative meaning, "I will not tolerate …" If Christians practiced Christ's message of toleration of the tax collectors, poor, lepers, blind, prostitutes, and sinners, rather than refusing to tolerate anything and everything that does not fit into the perfect, single-minded world and deity they have created, the faith might be growing in countries that can actually think and reason. Instead, it is growing in the countries that do not tolerate universal education, other races and religions, scientific facts, and even other humans who do not see the world the same way.

You know, even the Constitution, written only a couple hundred years ago, is open to interpretation. That's what the Supreme Court does. Though, if the court should rule against the closed-minded fundamentalist, the fundamentalist shouts that the court is legislating from the bench. He doesn't feel that denying individual rights is legislating from the bench, though—just judicial opinions that decide against his belief. Note, I do not say his knowledge, just his belief—a belief he has decided all people should hold at all times under all situations. He will not tolerate a differing opinion—reason be damned!

Other than actual, overt, physical violence, fundamentalist Christianity is a mirror image of radical Islam. One side blows people up and kills the body; the other destroys the spirit and mind and soul. More than anyone else, you, for example, have come the closest to convincing me that God may not exist. You have created a god that I would not be comfortable spending eternity with. You have created your personal friend who does not like anyone else nearly as much as he likes you. You have created a truth that fits for you, and you will not tolerate anyone else's insight into your personal, best friend. You have closed your mind to, and separated yourself from, not just the evil of the world, as in "come out from among them ... be a separate people," but, tragically, also from the truths of the world and the continual revelation of God. You seem not to tolerate God as God if his image goes against what you knew as a child.

Well, I guess that is what I think of intolerance: I am intolerant, too. I try to find the right for myself, and I try to tolerate others' beliefs as well. But what I am intolerant of is others forcing their views on others, especially when their views are unsupported by logic or truth and amount to myopic perceptions.

BIBLICAL MYTH

The following dialogue refers to an article about the potential schisms in various denominations that could occur because of new understandings and doctrines developing about homosexuality. The article also reported on potential changes in liturgical wording that would express less sexism in the language and offered experimental liturgies with alternative phrasings for the divine Trinity—"Father, Son and Holy Spirit." Among the possibilities: "Mother, Child and Womb" or "Rock, Redeemer, Friend."xxxiii

Eli: Now, what wacko's come up with this? Writing a new bible? Making up a new god? What will be the end of this ... Christ coming with a sword to wreak havoc on the lamebrains? How much clearer do I need to be to express disgust for this idiocy?

How about just going ahead and making up a new religion? It would at least be more sincere—so think I. I think the Presbyterians should join with the true Anglicans and throw the infidels out—give them no place in the leadership at all. Remember, I am a bigot, a biased and prejudiced fellow ...

Tell the backsliding bishops and mud-heads to repent and align themselves either with God or the devil—that is the final result. Tell them to get some self-control and quit acting silly.

Now, tell me, what do these guys think of the Bible? Is it just a summary of non-relevant myth, or do they see it as an "inspired of God" letter to us?

Jay: This is an example of how you seem to think the term *myth* applied to a part of the Bible is a put-down. I would think I have explained this sufficiently by now, though. "These guys," as you say, would probably think that the Bible is inspired, but it is not meant to be read as a book written by God. The writers were just like writers today who are inspired, or preachers who are inspired. They express the truth of God as they understand it. Their understanding comes from minds that work according to their training and environment. Some minds are poetic and write beautifully; others are detail oriented and write factually; others are visionary and see the bigger picture of everything—even thinking of how the past, present, and future work together.

Eli: Well now, what is your take on the biblical story—myth—of Jesus as a boy, a student, dumbfounding the folks at the temple when he was a twelve-year-old? Was he being kind or otherwise while giving lessons to the ones looked upon as the most educated at the time by the leadership of the Pharisees?

Was Jesus out of order as he spoke unkindly to the scribes and Pharisees, the hypocrites of his time? Was that a good model to observe, in which there was a clash of the ungodly and godly, as defined by Christ and his disciples? Was the invasion from heaven in the person of Jesus a desired thing by God or an unwarranted happening?

Education is not the issue. Godliness versus his opposition is the issue in any form—truth versus error, light versus darkness. I offer one word of obvious observation: Education does not center in the academic community, though they think that it does. Education is the accumulation of information, understanding, and wisdom that is applied and applicable to the community, nation, and world. It is an irony that many who cannot do the work in the community, like a city, become the inspectors who grade the quality of those doing the work. That is just a thought from my point of view—just to keep the fire going.

Jay: I do not reject any of the Bible or the biblical stories, as you styled it. The parts that are myth are particular genres of literature. These myths are a part of the way men have been speaking and writing since the beginning of language. Man is a storyteller.

By the way, even if there were a flood—and there were several major historical floods—the story of Noah is mythic. It may be a myth that is true, but it is a shared story in many of the world's religions, and it demonstrates truths beyond the animals coming two by two. The gods being angry with their creation or upset because the people were too noisy, as the Sumerian-Babylonian myth goes, and a family escaping in a giant teacup, as in China, are both ways of explaining what happened and why the gods would destroy their creation.

Saint Augustine of Hippo, one of the fathers of the faith from the fourth century, even in his time approached the story of the ark as other than straightforward. Because of the existence of the animals on distant islands after the flood and the impossibility of them reproducing and swimming there after the waters receded, he said that they were re-created post deluge out of the earth, as they originally had been. Further, he believed the paired animals herded into the ark were a type or representation of the various nations that were to be saved in the future and were not put there as breeding pairs.[xxxiv] The validity of his interpretation is not the point here, though. Rather, it is that church fathers accepted the Bible and its stories as metaphorical or symbolic or mythic even in the time the faith was in its infancy.

Eli: To me, a myth is not truth … an addition to the truth … with a base possibly in legend that has been knowingly added to for the sake of drama and fiction: The Odyssey, Jason and the Argonauts, the tales of Hercules, the son of the gods. These are myths. They may be a corruption of the tales of Samson—so thought by some.

In any case, I see the Bible as the Word of God as originally given. The translations of the several societies, according to my Hebrew classes in seminary, are the product of the meanings of the words used as defined by the in-hand dictionary, the textual compulsion, and the school of training that prepared the translator(s) for the work at hand. In my few translating days, it was clear that many words in English could be acceptable for the thought process as defined by the text.

I am glad you do not reject any of it.

Jay: Myths are not lies. Even Jesus fits the mythic genre. (Incidentally, he uses parables, not myths, to convey truth without being factual.) Are you still with me? Hang on. Most all of the main religions have the "corn king" who dies and is resurrected. You may know Osiris in Egypt, connected to the inundations of the Nile that fertilize and bring new life each year, and Dionysus in Greek myth, who dies and resurrects in connection with fertility and wine.

The entire cosmic element of the death of seeds that are buried and come back to life in spring is mythic. This is one of the reasons some are so confident Jesus is the true God. As C. S. Lewis says, this great truth of one dying for the many inevitably was present from the foundations of the world and is echoed, however imperfectly, in the attempts man made to translate this truth throughout history. He says Jesus is the one true myth; it completes, consummates, in him. All the attempts of man to explain that which is unexplainable through stories, trying to put into words things that cannot really be put into words, culminate in the story of God's son.

The *Epic of Gilgamesh* is the first such writing we have extant.[xxxv] It is Sumerian-Babylonian and tells of the hero searching for eternal life, because the death of his friend shakes him.

He goes to the garden of Dilmun, past the flowers made of jewels, to the Noah character, who had been saved from the deluge the gods sent to destroy the world; one of the gods had taken pity and saved him and his family. Anyway, when Gilgamesh asks the ancient one how he can get eternal life, too, the ancient one says immortality is not for man (other than for him and his kin, who are there already), and he gives a gift similar to eternal life to Gilgamesh. It is the flower of perpetual youth. The serpent later steals it from Gilgamesh as he travels back to the realm of the living.

This is a myth. It seeks to answer the unanswerable questions—why do we die, how should we live, who are we, who controls the universe, and so on.

The creation story and the Garden of Eden likewise carry the elements of myth. Now, think. Knowledge of good and evil really comes from eating a piece of fruit off the tree of knowledge, as does eternal life from the tree of life? Why did Jesus die? Couldn't we all just have some fruit?

God doesn't require us to say the fruit is an apple (actually, it was a pear, I hear?). The idea of pride, of wanting to be as God and usurping the powers of the omnipotent, is part of the evil outlined for man—not picking a piece of fruit. However, could the myth be true? Sure. It's not nearly as powerful if we play it that way, though. You disobey me, you die! Of course, you do not die on "that day," as stated in the biblical warning, though the length of the "day" could be measured as loosely as the creation day and evening (a day defined without the sun or moon), but then we get into having to find rationale for other things continually. Why did God say "on the day you eat of it, you will surely die"?[xxxvi] They didn't, unless pregnancies and lives occurred without regard to time. Why do we have to fight the literary genre that offers truth in story form so that it is more easily spread and kept through oral tradition? It tells why we die, why the world is against us (weeds, thorns, and what they represent), and so on.

Eli: The story of Gilgamesh and Enkidu is, I also believe, a pre-Christ picture that could have come down from the time of Shem to the days of Abraham and been corrected by the revelation of God to the prophets unto us today.

Jay: I hadn't ever heard that some consider Gilgamesh or Enkidu to be a confused story from the time of Noah or that it could be about Samson. I thought Samson's story was more about Delilah and the haircut, or even the idea of the wars with the heathen. I'm not sure that works. The truths of the two stories that the myth is supposed to illuminate do not appear to be congruent. But, I do not mean the entire Bible is myth. It is composed of various literary forms.

Moses, the Ten Commandments, and the Exodus have mythic elements, but they represent a mixture of history and tradition; they are not really myth. The psalms, as you know, are songs, not myth. The books of the prophets are the calls to the people to return to the path; they are not myth, though the prophets may call on myth occasionally to strengthen the image of their argument.

The history books are history; proverbs are just what they say, Song of Solomon and Psalms likewise. They are all literary forms. Calling the psalms "songs" does not decrease their validity as praises, laments, and so on. Calling stories that carry the mythic literary elements "myth" does not destroy the intent of the book or story. It strengthens it; it broadens the scope. It does not even say the story is untrue. The story simply demonstrates a truth greater even than the literal meaning (which may itself be true as well).

Gospels are narratives, biographies written from the perspective of their authors, so we have different paradigms represented: the Jewish, the academic Greek, the spiritual.

Acts—a continuation of Luke's gospel, isn't it?—is a history of the beginning of the church. The epistles are letters to the various churches in Rome, Ephesus, et cetera, dealing with the local problems those cities or churches were having, though ultimately the collection of the letters tended to have universal application.

The entire Bible is relevant; I do not discount it. I see it as the true writing of that man or this man as he interpreted life and his world and was inspired by God. But I do not see it as inerrant; it was written, as well as copied several times, by other men. I do not believe that makes it wrong; I believe it makes it very much a communication that man can read. He needs to read it as man, though, with the recognition that his limitations were shared by those who wrote it. The Bible is not God! God is God.

Eli: Let's look at the beginning—Elohim, the one who is plural, or the plural, who is one. In the beginning, God created. The spirit of God brooded over the waters. God said. Originator-Father, Spirit hovered—got involved. The Word happened—God said. 1 John 5:7 says these three are one.

The Word of God became flesh. I believe the Word of God is Christ. As Logos and splitter of the silence, he came to us. I agree there were conferences in the first centuries of the church trying to work out what he was: man, spirit, demigod. I leave that. For me, it is easy.

In any case, I believe the Lord breathed and inspired the thought (word, desire, expression, impulse, or picture) into the ones he chose. Now, in the reading of the Word, I have to determine which part I believe and comply with, approve of, or allow to be consonant in my life.

Jay: You are presenting inspiration as a sort of supernatural, magic writing. Dante was inspired by Beatrice, but she didn't dictate *The*

Inferno; she inspired him as a muse. All writers, I suppose, have muses. The difficulty we have here is important. Channeling is when a dead person or a spirit takes over a living person, and that person then writes a message or plays the piano or paints a picture, ostensibly just as the controlling spirit would. I do not see God as possessing the body or mind of the biblical authors. You do. I see the term *inspired* as motivating. It is a difference similar to the one between the letter of the law and the spirit of the law.

We grow in our understanding of God. We can leave behind the milk of the word and move on to the meat (you know that quote, right?).[xxxvii] In other words, grow! If we place the Bible on a pedestal and make it the omniscient, omnipotent, and omnipresent, we are making an idol. "Know God," we say to people. Christians do not say the Bible will save you; they say Jesus did.

Christians do not say the Bible created the world; God did. Man just tried to explain how he did it through the Bible. But mankind did not have the words to tell the scientific or spiritual truths necessary to explain how and why he did it. We *had* to tell it in stories that our language and finite minds could deal with.

Remember, in the midst of this early church, that Peter and Paul argued, as did Paul and Silas. They were not always of one mind. They corrected each other. Even God had to provide the dream to Peter to convince him that what God has made clean, do not call unclean.[xxxviii] God, in essence, said to Peter the written word does not encompass all there is of him. God wants us to know him, not just know the Bible.

GOD AND GAYS

Eli: I want to know why those in opposition to homosexuality and the anti-biblical stance it presents are called homophobic. This is one of the freeze words I spoke of. Those against homosexuality are not necessarily afraid of homosexuals.

Jay: I think this is a valid question from the conservative side. I do not believe that a phobia or fear of homosexuality is necessarily present in all of those who condemn gays. Some conservative Christians are making legitimate attempts to adhere to the scriptures that speak against it. There are, however, many who do fear homosexuals and for that reason take up arms against them. Sometimes it is because they either recognize the homosexual inclinations they themselves have, or fear they may have, and thus protest against it to deny this part of their being. We continually witness this in the outing of ministers and politicians who have been vocal opponents of gays or gay equality. This is only some people, though.

I guess that what happens is the whole group of anti-gay or anti-homosexual activists, from preachers to football players, have simply been lumped together in a group, and that group is called homophobic. When there is not really a reason to discriminate against gays, it is easy to appear to fear homosexuality.

I know that many in my church are "Christian-phobic" and are embarrassed to identify as Christian to strangers, lest they be thought to be like Falwell or Robertson. That could be seen as an interesting phobia.

What do you think of these ideas? Harold Meyerson reports in the *Washington Post* that a fundamentalist Southern Baptist minister writes in his blog that more and more people in the scientific community are realizing that homosexuality has a biological basis. That fact will present problems to the conservative community, who categorize it as a choice. Further, contemporary society finds a discrepancy within a righteous and loving deity who tends to condemn part of his creation for being what he made them. It also pushes the limits of fairness, it seems, for one person to be commanded to use his sexuality and one condemned for doing the same thing in the way he or she was made—meaning gay, of course.[xxxix]

Eli: God is the creator of all, even the fool who says in his heart, "There is no God." Is this guy among those who intimate that, since we cannot live up to God's design, we will create our own design and try to live according to our own rules? I am curious.

Now, as I have said to you, even if there is a created inclination to same-sex attraction, the original intent as defined in the creation of mankind, to fill up the earth, has to do with procreation. That is not possible with sexual interworking between two of the same sex. Though a red-blooded American boy may want to have sex with every red-blooded American girl he meets, such behavior is called fornication or adultery, and it is forbidden in the Old Testament and New Testament alike. Self-control is the issue. Self-control is the issue with stealing, lying, and obeying the Ten Commandments and all the specifics of the Holy Spirit.

Jay: You seem to conveniently ignore the real question here. The red-blooded American boy is told he can only have godly sex with his wife, but you ignore the fact that same-sex companionship is denied to the gays who would not only find little happiness with one wife, or two hundred wives, but would experience in most cases actual repulsion sexually—just as you would with gay sex. The fact is that a homosexual may be living by all the same rules as the heterosexual but still is condemned for what he is. Or, if you say it is the sin that is condemned, not the sinner, the heterosexual, as Meyerson puts it, is commanded to follow his natural instinct for sex, but the homosexual is supposed to stifle his same inborn instinct for sex. This is a difference, and you cannot ignore it by just stating the overused injunction that one should just avoid sin. Both boys are genetically provided this sexual instinct, but one must deny it, and the other must likewise fulfill it? Not logical, or at least not fair.

Eli: Now, this person seems to need another look at Romans, chapter 3. "There is none righteous, no not one. All have sinned and come short of the Glory of God."

Does this guy get anything? Straight people are not free to follow their passions outside the parameters of marriage and self-control! Nor are those born as killers, stealers, drunkards, hateful, or arrogant—none of them are allowed to follow demonic or un-Christian passions! How does this man's brain work?

Jay: How does the brain work that adheres so adamantly to an inerrant interpretation of a god who accepted slavery and a book used to support segregation? It is a god before science, as even Meyerson says. Notice your caveat "outside the parameters of marriage." Again, you are ignoring the question of a seemingly capricious god, as Meyerson says, who creates homosexuals and then condemns them to hell if they practice it.

Eli: So, now, are you invoking him to bless debauchery? Remember the story—or myth, as you would call it—of Noah? The whole world was full of what was noted as violence! The whole world thought it needful and necessary, but there was one guy who pleased God. Only eight people sided on the right side, and now are we going to face the same again? Even in the days of Moses, "Who is on the Lord's side?" was called, and that day, many who were not died. So, what of this God who makes the rules, and the people who make up their own rules of life, purpose, and interpersonal action?

Say we are on a big cruise ship. The guy across the hall decides to go fishing and drills a six-inch hole in the floor of his stateroom and puts a line in the flow of inrushing water. Should I declare it none of my business? Should we allow the fisherman to adjudicate it to be none of our business? There needs to be no stated answer; it is obvious we ignore all the arguments of how his family deprived him of fishing as a child, how the police took away his fishing pole, or how he has awaited this fishing trip for so long, and he had to do the fishing using the guise of a Royal Holiday cruise!

Yes, there is a God. He so loved the world that he gave the price for all the dumb things done by all of us. Yes, he loves the writers of these pieces and wants us all to know him and live like him.

Recently, I heard of a general being chastised for saying that homosexuality is immoral; I don't know the general personally, but I applaud him. Drunkenness is wrong. Lying to your family is wrong. Stealing is wrong. Killing outside the due process is wrong. Murdering the unborn child for convenience is wrong. Having sex with animals is wrong, even if you love them, feel safer with them, or have a natural propensity toward them. Having sex with your brother or sister is wrong. A lot of things in life are wrong.

The question is on par with those asked by many friends I preach to, telling them that some things are the will of God and some are not. Some show and tell me they can eat glass without harm. I am willing to let them eat the glass and visit them in the hospital. I don't hand them the glass or encourage the act. Whether they are with me or alone, they have the ability to eat glass. Now, I still don't believe they were born to eat glass. There is no nourishment there, so why do it?

Come on! Get a life! If you put all the homosexual men on a great big island, in one generation, they would all be gone! No discussion, no ranting and raving about rights ... gone! Done! Whether they are in love or not!

Jay: That's funny. I bet if you put all the heterosexual men on a great big island for the same amount of time, they would all be gone as well. And if you say to put women on the island with the men, well, both islands have inhabitants who know how to procreate. It is just on one island the men would enjoy it, and on the other island, they might find it disgusting, but they still could produce offspring. Besides all that, whether you believe gays are born that way or choose that "lifestyle," wouldn't they still be popping into existence back on the mainland? Just asking. And, as far as nourishment is concerned, are not emotional and psychological nourishments as valuable to the human being as food? They certainly are sought after. Thousands of volumes written are about romantic love and very few about meat and potatoes.

Eli: I say if having sex man-to-man is okay, so is sex with one's children, dogs, cats, and horses. Man-to-man sex is no more okay than is drunkenness, wanton killing, and every evil that is mentioned in the Bible, Old Testament, and New Testament. Anything that is outside the character or purpose of Christ in the creation is still outside the will of God. Simple.

Concerning lust, I know guys who are hot toward women! They want them all! So what? Get over it! Keep a cap on it! Do what you have to! Some have prayed, "God, blind me for your glory! Take me

from this body of sin and death! I don't like living! Too many girls look
so satisfying! This one is the one; this one will satisfy me. No … it is the
next one. No … the next one," and the torture is endless.

Jay: First, I don't advocate unbridled lust or sex, whether heterosexual
or homosexual. I think that man too often makes sex into a god or
a goddess and attaches entirely too much importance to it. True,
it is an extremely strong drive, second only to self-preservation, if
I recall correctly. I mean, if a lion and a naked woman are coming
at you, would you wait to have sex later and first escape from the
lion? Yeah, probably. But, if you are enamored and hot, you may
very well put off other activities or needs like eating, or bathing
(comfort), or finding someone to love you, or finding fame while
you exhaust yourself with sex. Thus, self-preservation seems to be
the only stronger drive.

I do not really think God is all that occupied with sex. Rather, he
concerns himself with how we treat others. If having several partners
were hurting a person, then it could be wrong. If it wasn't hurting
anyone, I would probably bow out and say that my job was to support
and not to judge another—unless of course it was my job to judge.
There is also a difference in judging the person and in defining an
action. I can say that a man who steals is not mine to judge ultimately
(other than deciding not to trust him with my car), but I can define
the action, stealing, as a wrong, because it hurts another.

If the theft turns out to be a case of survival, as in Hugo's
Les Miserables, I would have been hesitant to judge a man a thief
and sinner for stealing a loaf of bread off a windowsill to feed his
starving child. In a case like that, the real wrong, or sin, was the
selfishness and ignorance and lack of humanity of a society. That
society eventually fell—rather bloodily, too.

Further, the extension of my argument about homosexuality
to include incest, sex with animals, murder, and drunkenness is

not valid. Too many people try to lump being gay with pedophilia or these other actions, and it is not right. I am not arguing for any of those; I only argue for the position that what is interpreted as homosexuality in the various biblical ages, Old Testament and New, is not what we know and understand to be homosexuality today, and that we need to rethink what we have assumed wrongly to be God's words about it. Murderers and drunkards are not born that way; they become that way. The homosexual's very being is gay and will not change, just as the heterosexual cannot be separated from his inherent sexuality. This idea of being born gay is terribly important.[xl]

Just for some side reading, you asked for some data and authorities. This author I am dealing with now is a PhD in biology, I believe. I'll give you a link to an examination of his credentials later. I know you also said you don't care if homosexuality is natural or not, but I choose to ignore that side point for the moment, as it requires a different argument. I'll get more references for you when I have time, or you can simply follow Internet links found on the issue.

The problem, of course, is that you accept no authority but the Bible, and Jesus didn't really feel homosexuality was important enough to deal with, it seems. My coming arguments will deal with the authority question. My understanding of your position would be a bit clearer, perhaps, if you explain the reason you place the Bible in a place of inerrant authority. Take a quick look, also, at the book by Bart Ehrman, *Misquoting Jesus*.[xli] The first part deals with silly grammatical or interpretive errors, but the second part gets into the doctrinal issues that motivated purposeful mistranslations by the scribes based on their particular beliefs—not necessarily malevolent errors, just changes that would support the so-called orthodoxy they chose.

Erasmus of Rotterdam, a contemporary of Henry VIII and Sir Thomas Moore, bases the King James Version, which we love, on a Greek translation. (There are historical and translation errors that can be researched that were made by Erasmus.) Then we have the committee that made the King James Version from this translation. Moore, too, believed strongly in the biblical canon and died for it. He, however, interpreted the scriptures to indicate the pope as the only authentic head of Christ's church (even though the popes, and most of the clergy at the time, were pretty corrupt and political). So, both of you utilize the Bible as authority, but you, if I recall correctly, see the Catholic Church or pope as ungodly.

As to whether homosexuality is natural, you could read the book *Biological Exuberance: Animal Homosexuality and Natural Diversity* by Bruce Bagemihl.[xlii] In his work, he states that a large body of evidence and research proves that homosexual behavior (both male-male and female-female) occurs or is even common in at least 450 species, including representatives of birds and mammals. He concludes that such a presence in nature appears to support the idea that God thinks homosexuality is okay.

Eli: Are we just animals? In this fallen world, can we say homosexuality is normal, when nothing is normal as it was created?

Jay: Well, wait a minute. You can't use the argument that homosexuality is wrong because it just isn't natural and then turn around and say that we can't make a judgment based on simple observations of natural science, because nature isn't normal anymore. Other than that, the idea of global unnaturalness could be an interesting discussion point. It could be used to justify the notion that the homosexuality in the animal kingdom is not acceptable and just a result of the fall. Thus, the creation is spoiled, which we know it is. However, this proves problematic when used in man. The Bible says being this way is not acceptable; it does not just attack the actions. Therefore, one cannot justify oneself by simply not acting on one's homosexual inclinations—for example, living in a straitjacket, or joining a monastery, or entering the celibate priesthood. Even making oneself a eunuch would not change what one is. That means that the homosexual has no hope except for miracle, and those simply do not occur for everyone. It negates the sacrifice of Christ if one is a homosexual—no matter that he died, paid, substituted, forgave, or anything else—since the Bible says they will not enter the kingdom, if you will allow me that paraphrase.

Homosexuality is *not* an action. It is a state of being. The supposedly charitable Christians say that the church should welcome the homosexual and that he/she is a child of God, too, but those homosexuals may not live as who they are, or that would be sin. Well, that is a deceptive concession. It may keep the gay person quiet if this is believed, but it will not make them children of God in the sense of them being accepted by God.

You asked me why I had to "be right." This may be why. I cannot change who I am. If I were a thief, I could be forgiven what I had stolen in the past, and I would no longer be a thief. I could resist the temptation to steal; I would be a reformed thief. If I were a murderer, the same thing would be true. I know, you could say, "Once a thief, always a thief," but that isn't what we are dealing with. But, in the case of homosexuality, it is not a matter of stopping my actions. Were I to abstain from sex for ten years, I would still be a homosexual. If you stopped having sex with your wife, would you stop being heterosexual? This is an elusive point. I sense that it is not entirely clear to you yet. I am not putting you down for not seeing it; I am only trying to help you to see it.

In the case of homosexuality, there is no redemption according to your view of God. We are trying to get the world to understand that no matter how much or how long we want to change to heterosexual, it never happens. Sometimes we can stop all homosexual activity for our whole lives, but we are not changed to heterosexuals. The Bible does not just condemn the actions; it condemns the being. (Now, I am not dealing with miracles here; they may happen, but they have not happened to the millions of homosexuals).

The point is that the world is now capable of examining the phenomenon more than ever before, and we are discovering that human sexuality, while based in the preservation of the species, is far more complex and multifaceted than it was or is considered to be. There are, indeed, degrees of masculinity and femininity and of sexuality as well. God made the creation this way, and I do not think it is a mistake. The family of man, past and present, has not understood it yet. The Old and New Testament writers had to write from their perspectives. They spoke truth as they knew it.

Eli: The hedonism of the playboys and their magazine, is that normal? Acceptable? To be done as the example for society? I think not. Ask the children who are born out of wedlock, the girls who are not cared for by a loving husband or father who will be faithful to his promise to raise a child in a safe, secure, loving, and permanent family-covenant relationship. Even prostitutes often ask their partners, "Do you love me?" So, what is the definition of love—only the desire for the night, or the covenant that lasts a lifetime?

Jay: Is hedonism or being a playboy good? I doubt it, also. My definition of love is to desire the other's good. Selfishness is what we overcome the most in love, but, because of Eros, especially, it is also the sin that we most readily fall into. The asking of, "Do you love me?" is the strongest echo in humanity. It is never really fulfilled, though with Eros, it sometimes is covered over with pleasure.

Loneliness is man's condition without completeness. We are only complete when we become one, as the Father and Son are one. This either has not occurred yet, or we are not able to experience this oneness yet. I am not sure which, really. When we get to heaven, we will be as the angels: neither male nor female, or so the Bible says.[xliii] I think the separation of the sexes is really illustrative of the separation of our selves somehow, but that is another discussion.

Recall the statement that extensive research indicates homosexual behavior occurs or is common in at least 450 species, and that this seems to support the idea that God thinks homosexuality is okay.

Eli: Now, who in the world said this? It is beyond even responding to. The earth is fallen in sin. The car has been crashed. It is not as it was designed or created. The sin of man brought in sin and death to the whole creation. Now, we are to use the fallen creation as the standard or example for us to follow? Christ, the Redeemer, has what, gone on a failed mission? I don't think so! Show me where Jesus said the scriptures were wrong or too old to believe. I came not to destroy the law, but to fulfill it, he said.[xliv] *I did not come to rip up the check; I came to cash it!*

I am not impressed at all with those in evolution and philosophy who support the notion that God is on a long journey or his word is obsolete or a joke.

Jay: I am not one of those who see God as on a long journey, as the watchmaker, or as a deist philosophy. Nor do I believe the Word (herein meaning Bible) is obsolete or a joke. I have never said either of these things. There is a point here, though. I fear that you and many others interpret biblical criticism and evolution theory as representing this philosophy. True, some people do this, but not all. The Bible or any book is enhanced by what we bring to our reading. The well-known and true saying is, "You only get from a book what you bring to it." Don't carry that too far to the extreme, though. It only means we see with the spectacles we have on. The cleaner and the better-prepared spectacles enable us to perceive better.

Eli: You know where I have made my bed. When a person has a bias and gets all available information to prove that point, how far away is that from being a bigot? University bigots and church bigots … still bigots. Biased, prejudiced.

Jay: Could we strive to not be bigots but rather to be seekers of truth? There is a difference between being faithful to one's friend and just being faithful to one's image of one's friend. I want to see more clearly. I do not know the answers; I only long to find them. I want to know God better, not have to prove he has not changed from my first images of him.

Eli: I read an article I would like you to give a comment about, if you would. The article was about a hearing on the 1992 Colorado Amendment 2, passed by the voters. It mandated that no public agency or government in the state could pass any ordinances or laws that would grant equal rights, or special rights, or special protections, to gay or lesbian people.

The writer of the article said that during the public testimony on the issue, he shared an anecdote intimating that all lesbian people had suffered physical, sexual, or emotional abuse from a man in their past. He then said that he believed all gays and lesbians have suffered from an unprotected childhood or youth due to the absence of a protective father. This makes them especially sensitive to the terms used in the amendment—terms like "special rights" or "protected status." He concluded that sensitivity probably comes from the lesbians never feeling protected or special. He heard moans and groans from the lesbian audience during this part of his testimony. He went on to say that the unfortunate wordings, like "special" and "protected," are inflammatory to gays and are even beginning to motivate very large donations from wealthy gays to gay-friendly politicians. He concludes that this is becoming troubling.

What do you think about this evident sense of loss expressed by the gay community during his testimony? Are these bad word choices?

Jay: I do not believe the moans and groans would have been generated from the lesbians' identification with, or any reminders of, pains in their past, as the writer intimated. Nor, as the story seems meant to imply, did their past treatment cause them to be homosexual, nor are they objecting to the language of the amendment ensuring that they should receive no rights that would make them "special" because they were not "special" as young people.

More likely, the implication that abuse had been a causal agent of their homosexuality and the argument that gays want "special" rights not granted to the general populace motivated the groans. They do not seek special rights. They ask, for example, to receive the thousand-plus rights that come only with a signature on a heterosexual marriage license. Those entering into gay unions, on the other hand, have to pay attorneys to provide things like power of attorney, visiting rights for hospitals, wills, guardianship papers, partnerships, and so on. The gay marriage may be anathema to Christians, but it does not provide special rights—only equal rights to those who wish to commit themselves to an enduring relationship with the ones they love.

Gay people likewise do not accept that it is a "special" right that an employer cannot fire them for simply being who they are. Homosexuals do not accept that protection from housing discrimination is a "special" right, or that equal protection under the law is asking for "special protection." These are basic rights and protections that a citizen might reasonably expect. These rights would include protection from physical abuse or even death. Yes, being beaten to death is not at all uncommon, and it can occur for no other reason than a person is identified as gay. Notice gays and lesbians are subject to this persecution always, not just at times when they may be holding hands or kissing on the street, as straight people regularly do. Discrimination isn't limited to gays who dare to show affection in public; gays suffer discrimination just for being gay.

The argument made in the article about the moans and groans is so far off base it is pathetic. What the guy is really saying is that the language in this amendment, calling basic rights "special," indicates all too clearly the bias from which they are really preaching. The writer doesn't see at all the gays' point that equal rights and protection are not considered "special" to the lesbians. These attempts to maintain a status quo permitting discrimination are making too many people angry—even very wealthy people, who are now financing friendly political candidates. This historical discrimination is also bringing other human-rights groups to the gay cause, and it is even grating on straight people's consciences. More and more people are coming to realize that homosexuality is not a danger to the tribe, but it is and always has been a natural part of the human condition.

You know, the sad thing is, I tend to think the writer actually believes what he was saying and doesn't see what he was really implying. That probably doesn't make sense to you, does it?

Eli: What makes sense is to follow what the Bible clearly says.

Jay: I think I have the answer to the gay question! You believe that gays, even though God may have made them that way, are still just like all the other sinners and should stop sinning. That of course means they must be celibate or try to have sex (if they are a man) with a woman, which to them might be a bit like having sex with a doll.

So, they will then have to conclude—since the only sex they can even participate in without cringing is with their own physical gender—they must then be celibate, as any sex (not to mention the requisites of loving, holding, kissing, consoling, et cetera) they could enjoy or even endure would be a sin. Very well: if having sex is a sin, be celibate. Yes, others in the world have done that. I know the Catholic Church agrees that all priests should be celibate, though not necessarily all parishioners.

This follows the admonition that if your brother sees eating meat used as offerings to idols as a sin, then you (who know it is not really a sin, even though the scriptures say it is) should abstain from eating the meat offered to idols, too.[xlv]

I bet the gays would listen if you and all the other literalists would publicly abstain from sex for your entire lives as well. That would show your love and concern for your weaker brethren. They could then say, "Wow, if the whole world of heterosexuals can abstain from sex with the ones they desire, maybe I can, too!"

It would even be fair. Everyone would be equal, and the "haves" would not just be telling the "have-nots" that that is what God wants only for gays. The haves would be showing the have-nots that they can abstain from the meat as well.

What do you think? Meanwhile, until this has spread among the saints, we will just tell the gays to go on their way, sin not, and be well fed and clothed, as the Bible condemned the pseudo-saints for doing in their failed care of parents?[xlvi]

You never answer any of the arguments with arguments, facts, reasoning, or logic. You only quote the Bible. Is that all there is to man? Is that all he is expected to do—just read the Bible and not use his brain, or feelings, or logic, or history, or science? Why the heck are we here if we are just automatons? God could make angels to sing his praises, if that's all he needs; they have better voices than I do anyway.

Eli: My task in life is to become more and more like Jesus, not try to make him more and more like me. I am for righteousness and truth from his point of view, and I try to abandon my past, not try to make him like my past. I want holiness, not to have Jesus in the mire of my passions; I want to be in his passions. I don't plan to change that desire, no matter how much information comes at me to the contrary. That is bigotry. I don't plan on changing that position.

Jay: Again, you hit the nail on the head: the problem is the nail is a screw, and you are still not able to accept that. Try to be calm.

All that is, of course, what I already knew, so your response held no real surprises. I really do understand where you are at and why you are there, and I defend your position as well. When I discuss our ongoing debates with others, I am comfortable in defending you and telling them you truly do believe all you say with all your heart and always have. I understand your inability to change that as well. Actually, I am not that different from you, even though it seems so to you.

My difference does not require less belief in God or Jesus, or even the Bible. I just see it from a literary point of view and with historical paradigms intact. We simply see God requiring different "goods." And there are different goods; I don't mean to change basic laws, so don't get too upset with that.

As for bigotry, no information coming to you would necessarily have to change your basic Christianity. The only change I argue is the interpretation of truth and righteousness that you see Jesus or the Bible as having. I see the teachings a bit differently from you. Remember, he said we would do even greater things than he, because he was going to the Father.[xlvii] We then have duties we are fulfilling, and I do not think he meant just the number of people we talk to. He wasn't overly concerned with that. I think he meant that we would be able to find answers to much of the evil (like disease, poverty, et cetera) in the world—even that we would learn more about the Father and the universe.

Eli: Look at Acts 15. There are in the New Testament things forbidden— among them, fornication. What is that? How does it fit the homosexual and heterosexual discussion? Is it okay for a homosexual to do it and a heterosexual not to? No, it is forbidden. Does it happen in and out of the church community? Yes. Is it smiled upon by the Boss? I don't think so. What do you think?

I am a bigot ... I am not going to change in my belief that the Bible is the Word of God. Are you going to quit believing homosexuality is inborn? Are you going to start believing it is a decision—a small, minute decision?

Jay: You say the Bible is the Word of God. Fine, we won't argue that, but you pair that with the statement that homosexuality is a choice. Is it a choice we make, like saying, "Hey, toddler, do you want to be gay or straight as you live your life?" If this were the case, for what reason would anyone choose homosexuality? Or ...

Eli: The choice becomes a concern after the realization that said choice is taboo. Then it is called sin, choice, stealing, coveting, adultery, fornication ... killing without due process and the acts of war ...

Jay: Or, is it that we are born homosexual or heterosexual, but we must then choose to allow only heterosexual feelings and actions? This appears to be what the church wants. Those who condemn homosexuality as being perverse and against God say they accept the homosexual as a person, as a friend, and as a fellow sinner, but they do not accept his or her acting on the fact of what they are. Does this "love the sinner, not the sin" almost hint they are born that way?

Eli: No, all are born with DNA. All are born with human sin and are woeful.

Jay: Oops—you need to tell me what "woeful" is.

Eli: All have a sad story: I am misunderstood, I should be allowed an extra dispensation, I am special, I am different. I should be allowed murder, fornication, adultery, covetousness, and so on.

Jay: But, if you say they are not born that way, we are left with the homosexual sitting in the church, choosing to live as only part of a person, unable to love or enjoy love's expression. Again, if it is a choice, why on earth would anyone choose to live a life like that? It doesn't make sense!

Eli: Do you know of anyone who screams that their problem, habit, twist, or uniqueness is not their fault: cleft palate, twisted face, elephantitis, cancer? The world is a world that is in the process of being redeemed at the return of Christ. 'Til the time this mortal puts on immortality, we must deal with what is … what we ache to put off … this physical body and the claims made to it by the fallen world. I think we all have overt and covert wars fought in and out of view of others. The problem is we are not the creators or the solution to the problem. God set the rules, and Adam and Eve did the deciding. Eve was deceived; Adam made the decision that has bound all who are his descendants. Until Christ does his thing and comes again, we are stuck in the meantime. I choose to have hope it will be worth it—choose.

Am I always good at choosing? Obviously, no. So, the word repentance *comes into play. I get to do it daily. He is merciful, kind, and forgiving. I take advantage of it.*

Jay: I recognize your reference to this world groaning to be made perfect. Still, this argument presents many problems with my way of thinking. First, I do not think being born gay is a sickness— nor does the medical, psychological, social, or even much of the theological community. Being born blind or with a cleft palate, or getting leprosy or cancer all represent violence placed on a person. Homosexuality is simply a biological fact, not a disease or disability. There are perfectly healthy, well-adjusted, intelligent people who are also gay and live a perfectly sane and healthy life. They simply are equipped with a sex drive that is not the same as many others.

The gay man or woman is not a mistaken creation (and no, I do not believe God creates blind people, either). The crippled and the blind are not condemned in the Bible for being crippled or blind, except of course in Leviticus. They are not told they are abominations or forbidden to walk because they have to walk with a limp—although the lepers in biblical times were considered to have brought it on themselves a good portion of the time and had to separate themselves and call out "unclean" as they walked, begging for alms. I do not believe God makes human beings gay as a test or a punishment. Homosexuality is simply part of the creation itself. It isn't a fallen state at all. It is just one of the myriad elements making one person different from another.

You seem to believe that the Bible says homosexuality is a choice, and that it is not how one may be born. Where does it say that?

Eli: It lists the action of homosexuality as combined with sins such as killing, stealing, lying, and adultery. All are forbidden—sin, something the character of Christ abhors.

Jay: In about six places, the Bible mentions homosexual acts but not necessarily what we know as homosexuals today. In Romans, homosexual lust is described as a punishment visited on those who deny God or don't worship him properly. (That is a very strange sort of punishment, by the way.) But it doesn't seem to me that it is said to be a choice and not a fact at birth, as you say.

You may have one mate you love. I may not have one I love. If you then say I may have one woman to love, I would have to respond that you, then, could have one man to love. Are these parallel? Would you go for it? Just having sex without romantic love is not what I want, and that is what we would have if I were with a woman, or you were with a man.

Eli: What if a man were married to the wrong woman? They were in love at first and then fell out of love later on. Then the supposedly right woman came along. Is it okay to practice adultery, to have sex (maybe on the side) just to relieve the hunger for loving sex? Is adultery okay, good, acceptable? Or is it still breaking one's word, still changing one's mind—a wrong, a covenant breaker? Is it sinful behavior that misses the mark of the character of Christ?

And here you and I are—in a world we did not ask to be born into. Do we have to live by rules we did not vote on? Must we obey this eternal God just because he is God, and he makes the rules and not us? Is that fair, or is it just the way it is? Wouldn't it be great to have ten wives, one to do the finance, another washing, another kissing, another ... until they all start fighting and won't quit! Then one wife seems better.

Jay: I think your argument about the man falling out of love has a bit of validity. We see this continually in society. It sounds good on the surface: man needs love, and if it is no longer present in a relationship, can he move on? Is this parallel to the homosexual question of being allowed to be in a love relationship? This presents two different issues. The one we are supposedly debating is, is it possible that gays, like straights, have a right to fulfill the basic human need for a loved one, a partner. You argue two paths. If the gay chooses that lifestyle, it is against God's wishes and therefore sin outlawed by the Bible. If the gay is born that way (which you do not really prefer), homosexuality is like a birth defect and simply has to be lived with, and the victim must simply learn to, metaphorically, walk with a limp or not at all.

This question of falling out of love and deciding if it is right to then leave the relationship to find love with another is not the issue we are debating. It is perhaps worthy of debate, but I'm not arguing that one now. You haven't allowed that gays can enter into a love relationship in the first place, so there is no need to argue whether they or straights can justifiably leave it. I would say now, however, that this concept contains deeper levels for consideration than you are assuming. I think this question demands an examination of what is right and wrong—or, in your terms, what is sin. Again, we differ on this question as well.

I understand your position is to take the Bible as the direct command of God and obey it unquestioningly, even if it appears to contradict what we see as moral or right. I, on the other hand, feel it is necessary to look at what the Bible says as being filtered through man, the various writers of the Bible, and the cultural mores of earlier civilizations with differing levels of understanding about the human being and his society. I present the treatment of women, slaves, prisoners of war, and the enemies of the Jews in much of the Old Testament as examples of how even you have rejected the Bible as the final authority on keeping slaves, on charging interest to gentiles but not to fellow Jews, or even on killing enemy babies and women during war.[xlviii] But perhaps I am wrong. Maybe you do accept these mores, perhaps especially during the Cold War and the wars on terrorism.

I think God presented his rules and dictates to help man reach the good, and if a dictate seems to go against a good—like killing the innocent children, as even God supposedly did in the flood of Noah's time, or condemning the woman if she is raped in the town, but not condemning her if she is raped out of town—we should use our God-given intellect to find the good in the dictate. I think that God is good, and whenever we find the good, we find God.

You seem to say that God wants us to be good, but he decides what is good even if it goes against what he has said is good. The murder of babies is an example. To me, then, good is what is truly commanded, regardless of the words some man has written down, and God is good. To you, good is relative to what God supposedly says at a particular time—sometimes the murder of babies is good?

I wonder how you would react to the denying of basic rights to women or even prisoners of war. The controversy over the United States torturing prisoners and the brouhaha about the treatment of prisoners at Guantanamo, in Cuba, is a good example. I mean, the world, for the most part, agreed on certain rules of decency, even during war, when most all countries admitted the accords of the Geneva Conventions.

Eli: I have no opinion of the prison in Cuba. Some may not need to be there; some do. I am on the bias bar, anti almost everything to do with ACLU; I am more pro ACLJ. I think the same toward ACLU as the group Move On ... whose information I get weekly. If someone were going to blow up my family, I would count it a joy to torture someone until they told me where the bomb existed. What if this is the wrong captive? Find out. If we cannot find out, we do what we must and take the risk of doing wrong or right to save the life of our loved ones. What do you think?

Jay: So, is there no Bill of Rights or protections for the citizen or the prisoner or another human being? Just what is it, then, that makes the United States better than other nations, or even worth defending, other than the fact that you and your family presently live here? This interrogation technique—or torture, if you will—works fine if the president or the general is on your side, but what if the jailer or interrogator is not on your side, and he decides to torture your family because he thinks your wife is a terrorist? So, they hold her, and your son objects, so they ship him off to the "residences" in Afghanistan or Germany or wherever and torture him to make him turn in his mom?

Eli: Schwarzkopf said, "War is hell." Are we still "at war"? Does that matter? In war, the inhuman and unimaginable are done. In WWII, soldiers told of shooting the heads of the Japanese who were hiding in holes as the Allies came ashore to destroy the enemy. It was hateful and brings flashbacks even years, decades later.

Jay: It seems to me we are always at war, so, hell or not, I'm not accepting war as a valid argument. I could have sworn that at some time in your life, you took an oath to uphold the Constitution of the United States from all enemies, foreign and domestic. The rights granted by that document are broken all the time. I don't understand. What is it that you are living for, just your family? I suspect that isn't really the case. You are out preaching to others all the time, all over the world, so you have to care about others—unless you are doing it only to save yourself at the apocalypse.

I tend to think the United States at one time had a soul and a conscience. Now we can just screw with whoever we want, innocent or guilty, if we think the person might possibly be guilty? If one uses the argument that the criminal didn't respect the rights of his victim, so he should not be granted any rights in his interrogation to determine his innocence, one misses the point that he is *not* a criminal until he is proven to be one. Otherwise, why bother to even find the guilty one? Let's just go around torturing everyone. I'm sorry, but you are wrong.

Eli: I like the cute way you make a straw man and then take aim and beat it to death. War is not pretty, not desired. It gives nightmares. Who likes Guantanamo? I don't. Is it necessary? I am not commander in chief.

Jay: Oh, balderdash! Discussing the punishment of the innocent before proving him guilty is not a straw man. The morality of such behavior is exactly what we are arguing. You said you would joyfully torture the man you have in custody because he may have information on a bomb that would blow up your family. Whether he is innocent or guilty makes no difference to you. This is why we have the rule of law. You can't just throw the laws out when you want, or there is no reason to have laws. One cannot play chess if the players can always take back their moves later in the game. It may pass the time, but it isn't chess! Now, if the law is bad, we need to change the law. And, in essence, that is exactly what I am arguing in our present topic. The Bible's judgment of gays and the conservative's perception of gays require rethinking.

I agree that we need to discover the truth as quickly as possible to deter terrorist attacks, or any attacks. I do not advocate televisions, and steaks, and cocktails for the prisoners. We must treat them as human beings, though. That is what we signed on to with the Geneva Conventions. Statistics appear to indicate that even though torture works sometimes, it is not a reliable method. I have read Tom Clancy's novels and recognize his arguments, and in the heat of my anger and hatred for the fictional foe (who, because of the way the story is told, I *know* is guilty), I am anxious to see him destroyed—brutally, if necessary. But I am not proud of those feelings.

With all due respect, the fundamentalist, Islamic terrorists are doing exactly what you are advocating: they destroy the guilty and the innocent, all for the name of God and their beliefs.

There is an excellent essay by C. S. Lewis titled "God in the Dock."[xlix] The "dock" in the title is the prisoner dock in court. Prior to his death in 1963, Lewis discussed the phenomenon that we no longer place ourselves under the judgment of God, but instead place God in the dock for our judgment.

This may sound blasphemous, but if we did "eat of the fruit of the knowledge of good and evil," we had best employ that knowledge, hadn't we? And we should use this knowledge not only in the judgment of the supposed attributes of God, but in the writings of the canon.

If we do not, we then deny the attributes supposedly inherent in the fruit. If there really were no attributes, like the knowledge of good and evil that Adam and Eve could gain from the fruit, then the Garden of Eden story was a lie, and God is punishing mankind for a crime not really committed. If God is punishing us for a lie, and the fruit did not contain the knowledge of good and evil, why would we need propitiation for that supposed sin? Unless, of course, that mythical god were simply an example of might makes right—a belief civilized people tend to repudiate.

There will always be those who do not grow in the knowledge of God and truth. They will be easier to identify in the future, and we need the fundamentalist interpretations and the deified Bible to exist alongside the liberals. It is easier to distinguish the truth when we have versions to compare—just as we view the Jerry Falwells and Pat Robertsons in contrast to the Presiding Bishop of the Episcopal Church and other spokespeople of the so-called liberals.

VIEWPOINTS: SIN, SEX, AND HISTORY

Jay: Let's look at the story of Jonah and the whale—or the big fish, if you will. Jonah does not want to preach to the Ninevites in the first place, and then when he finally gets out of the fish, he agrees to it. He preaches, and then the Ninevites repent, and God decides not to destroy them after all. Jonah is not pleased and pouts in the shade of a plant. Then God sends a worm to destroy the plant and Jonah's shade. I see this as an allegorical story demonstrating a larger point. Did Jonah need to see things differently? Does that explain the plant and the worm?

Eli: Yes, he needed to see the grand mercy of God. The mercy came when the king and nation repented. It came when the Ninevites complied with what they knew was true: that they should be righteous and godly. Then they repented. God wanted Jonah to see that God does not want to judge but to see his creation doing justly and living in a godly manner. So, he did not tell Jonah at once. God just let him wonder what was going on. Why did God not do it in forty days? As Jeremiah 18 says, God is merciful ... and is slow to anger ... you know it.

Jay: Jonah's excuse to God as to why he ran in the first place existed because he already knew God was merciful. Your argument takes it to a different place. Is he hesitant then because preaching would be a waste of his time, or because if he preached and the destruction did not happen, he would be killed as a false prophet?

I think there is a third possibility. I recall a discussion in one of my theology classes that presents an interesting historical context. The story of Jonah, like the story of Ruth, is a literary creation written after the exile—somewhere in the time of Ezra and Nehemiah, I understand. As do many short stories coming out of this time period, both Ruth and Jonah carry a pretty strong message. Postexilic Judah was going through a xenophobic stage, trying to bring about pure-blooded Jews again. The author of Ruth realized the exiled and fallen Jews had perceived intermarriage between Jews and gentiles, in the past as well as during the exile, as one probable cause, a scapegoat, for the Jewish captivity. Marrying outside the "chosen people" thus precipitated the loss of power for the Chosen and their God.

This xenophobia was breaking up many families, and, like all so-called cleansing movements, it seemed to engender protests. Compare it with the Aryan cleansing centuries later. One of the actions of protest was the writing of these stories. The ending of the book of Ruth sort of creeps up on the unsuspecting reader or listener. There the genealogy shows us that the foreigner, Ruth, was necessary for the house of David to even exist—sort of a gut punch to the xenophobia and ethnic cleansing going on at that moment.

By demonstrating Jonah's "concern" for the plant more than for the people, this story evoked conversation and thought among the people about the ethnic cleansing going on in their own time. Actually, as a real-life character, Jonah is a bit strange, isn't he? He "works for" God, yet he won't go to Nineveh to preach for their coming destruction because he believes God is merciful and will forgive them. This sort of fits with the idea of the ethnic-cleansing group, as if he, too, might be xenophobic and did not want the Ninevites saved, doesn't it? Then, when he is pouting and sitting outside the city, God has to demonstrate that all people, not just the "chosen people," have value to him, and maybe the Jews should not persecute them through ethnic cleansing. Anyway, Jonah is not a very nice guy, at least to me. He does, however, have a lot of courage to say no to God and then pout like a spoiled child.

Pay attention to the point I would like to make, though. Jonah had to rethink his position on a people whom he hated or feared or even ignored. God used the plant to illustrate that sometimes our minds need to be changed. If God is more merciful than Jonah, and he accepts the people, maybe man should, too. As far as the people accepting the story as total fact: well, the worm and plant grew really fast, didn't they?

But the Bible seems to rather cavalierly ignore physical laws, whether in botany or physics. Look at the time/light of the universe, for example. The creation story must stretch the laws of time and space—consider the passage of light-years that must occur for the light of stars to reach us. Ought we to make God create all the physical laws just to break them, so he can confuse us?

Eli: Psalms does say he spread out the heavens. Does that make the stretch or spread observable—scientifically, that is? So, what so troubles you about the only God doing something miraculous, like making everything in six twenty-four-hour periods?

If he is going to speak, to use so little effort as to speak, why should it be a big deal for it to be fast? What kind of a god takes a rock, leaves it for a trillion years, and has a man? If the Bible said that, so be it. But, it says "twenty-four hours" in Hebrew. Yom *denotes a day: twenty-four hours, the evening and the morning—even more scientific than the trillion-year theory.*

Hey, did you know that when the Darwinists voted that there was no god (small g), they took the bold statement that the universe had been around for about seventy thousand years? Wow, a long time! Much longer than six thousand years the Bible indicates. Hey, now the guys say three and a half billion! Isn't it tremendous how the guessing community of atheists has increased the timeline? It takes a long time to get from a rock to a man if there is no God!

Jay: As I have said before, I am not too concerned with this issue. Many theories, creationist and evolutionist alike, have become twisted around in peoples' minds, and none of them are anything I would be able to prove one way or another, anyway. The idea of one day—evening and morning, twenty-four hours—being "scientific" is sort of droll to me, however. God had not created the sun and moon for the first evening and morning, or the second or the third. It was only on the fourth day that there were two great lights to govern the day and the night and to separate light from darkness. Likewise, there were no lights in the skies to mark seasons and days and years until the fourth day, either, though there was light and darkness. This gives me pause in determining evening and morning, though I am sure one could have "stretched" the heavens to answer this.

Now, there is another possibility that I have considered. Perhaps days and seasons and years are actual "things" and are neither created nor measured by linear time as we know it in this universe. Then, when God says he gave the sun and moon and stars as signs of the seasons, or to govern the day and the night, we can assume they are not really the cause of the daylight or darkness, nor of the definition of day or night. They are just a means of measurement for mankind. One might be able to wrench this interpretation out of the translated Bible, but it seems an awfully contrived explanation. The simpler is better to me.

Recent news: the world's telescopes, just by chance, caught a supernova explosion of a star as it occurred, a one-in-infinity chance. But the light rays of that explosion seen by the telescopes actually took somewhere around eighty-six million years to get here, if I recall correctly. According to your stretching theory, the supernova would have only occurred six thousand years ago and would have been "created" in the supernova death stage, along with the billions of other stars that have exploded leaving only their remnants today. Likewise, the white dwarf stars or the red giants—which, if I recall correctly again, are the remainders of stars at various stages of their lives—would have been "created" in their death throes. Does this not even strike you as odd? If we are in the fourth day of creation, sin and death have not entered the universe; why create dead and dying elements of the universe?

Also, I do not see how the fact that the Darwinists, as you call them, have changed their estimate from seventy thousand years to three and a half billion years indicates a "guessing" community. The scientific community operates on the current knowledge. As new evidence presents itself, scientific understanding broadens, and adjustments become available to the public and other scientists. Science is an ongoing search for accuracy and truth. Scientists do not just hold to their first theory or hypothesis and make every new truth fit into the old wineskin.

Truth is not present only at one time or in one form. What was at one time excellent wine in theory turns to vinegar after a while, and one needs to accept new wine, made with fresh, newly grown and picked grapes. Even biblically, that new wine, of course, requires new wineskins. By the way, since the scientists started using the Hubble telescope, they date the origin of the universe at more like fourteen billion years ago. This means (considering the speed of light) we can see what was happening fourteen billion years ago at a given point in the universe.

Eli: You know, you uphold the physics and astronomy laws very well, always arguing for them as facts, but you criticize the spiritual and religious laws. Why can't they be lifted up as well? When I join the fight to push, say, the Ford Company into agreement with biblical law, instead of encouraging gays to pretend to marry and have families as men and women do, you get upset and bring up the Pharisees. So, just how does the Ford boycott by Christians fit into the story of the Pharisees? Ford's management supported the nonsense that a family could be defined as gays who are just living together and having sex. Give me a take on this. What is the parallel?

Jay: I see your limited definition of family. I will lodge a side protest here that a family is not just a man, wife, and child amalgam. What if the wife is dead? Is it no longer a family? But let's get back to the original matter at hand.

First, let me broaden the label of Pharisees to include the Sadducees and even the priestly classes, for the sake of simplicity. We are not concerned with the delicacies of the Pharisees' various doctrines but with the fact that they represented the leadership of the Jewish religion during the time of the historical Jesus. The biblical impression of them was not positive. The parable of the Good Samaritan shows a victimized traveler passed by, for example, as he did not meet the religious purity regulations.[i] Healing people on the Sabbath or picking corn to eat on the Sabbath (both of which Jesus did) were grounds for persecution by the church because of the "laws," which really were the rules of the church, written and read continually.

Jesus castigated the religious for practicing the rules of godliness and forgetting why the rules were there. The Sabbath was made *for* man, not man for the Sabbath, he says. He rebelled at the idea that people prayed in public for the eyes of the public—to be seen and admired for their holiness—rather than going into the closet, where God, who sees in secret, can reward openly.[ii] He showed that God does not believe the outward show of godliness when it ignores the very essence of God: love mercy, walk uprightly, and live justly.

Notice that Jesus is not telling them to follow the written rules, but to follow the greatest two commandments.[lii]

The idea that the religious class was demanding a righteousness of the people that even the priests themselves could not reach was appalling to Jesus as well. He scoffed at swallowing a camel and straining at a gnat. Jesus accepted the creatures of God, attacking none but those who were supposedly acting for God and giving God a bad name. He did not advocate sin; he did not advocate the negative; he spoke for the positive. If one loves one's neighbor and one's God, one will not have trouble with sin. It is quite simple. The real law will be written on the heart. This does not mean that we will not have to seek answers to difficult problems, however. Growth is a physical, mental, and spiritual process.

The Ford incident and the gay question serve very well as illustrations of these different systems of God's law. If I recall correctly, you were an advocate for the boycotting of Ford products, thus attempting to put the Ford Motor Company out of business. The reason for this boycott was that Ford's union and shareholders lobbied the company to provide health insurance to cover cohabitating partners not married by the state. I put it this way rather than saying "married gays" because of the legal terms involved. The issue would have covered—or not covered, as the case may be—the unmarried heterosexual couples who were living together as well as homosexual marriages and partnerships would be my guess. That is normally the case. Ford had complied with this, and the fundamentalist movement felt this was unacceptable and thus sought to punish Ford by putting the company out of business.

God is not a big brother one can sic on someone or something one does not like. If the boycott had succeeded—which it did not—what would have happened? What would have been good and bad? First, the workforce of tens of thousands of employees of the company itself, Christian fundamentalists included, would have been unemployed. This would have placed huge burdens on financially strapped, uneducated families who heretofore had had a job that paid well.

This newfound poverty would lead to family stress, which could lead to family and personal problems that could lead to all sorts of evil within the community. The same would happen to thousands of others. The problem would expand exponentially as these people lost the ability to buy goods, leading to shutdowns of other merchants and so on, like circles of dominoes falling outward. Would it be the end of the world? Of course not, but it would almost be for some people—mostly innocent ones.

And what would the boycott gain? Well, unmarried partners, gay and straight, would not be able to get medical insurance. Thus they would put off medical care, which could lead to more dangerous health issues and more potential burdens on society, which then must foot the bill for the uninsured's medical care. The suffering would go on and on.

I do not recall Jesus asking about the sexual history of those he healed. That was not the purpose of the healing. When he said "go and sin no more," an adjustment in sexual orientation was not his aim. The conservative, fundamentalist community could stand up and boast that they have lots and lots of power and can put a huge motor company out of business. They could say, "See what happens when you see sin differently from the way we see sin? See how we can harm millions of innocent people just to stop maybe five hundred same-sex partners from getting to see a doctor and having insurance pay for it? See how we can pray to our God, and he obeys?"

This is how I connect the Ford boycott and the Pharisee difficulties. The boycott is a street-corner prayer, or fight; it is ignoring the truth of the gospel for the rules made for man—and, too often, *by* man. It creates a camel out of a gnat, and it attempts to use God for one's personal purpose and not his purpose. This of course, will not happen. It assumes an understanding of God that he is the personal property of a certain group—which sets them aside as untouchable by sin and, even more unfortunately, by new wisdom and understanding. That is the great tragedy. Even Paul knows there is a difference between understanding as and speaking as a child and as an adult—between seeing clearly and obscurely.

Eli: Aren't you being a little self-righteous yourself? The gay community is just as rabid to boycott, or at least complain about, a company that presumes to discriminate against sin. How can what is okay for the goose not be okay for the gander? Why do you get to do that?

Jay: I think that is a valid question. Further, I would even say that there is truth to your claims. My hesitation would be based on some subtleties of the situations and the probable outcomes. First, when the gays withhold business from a company, they are not putting the company out of business. That is not the purpose. They are metaphorically voting—revealing a large number of customers who disagree with the company's stance and who think it is time for the business to rethink the relevance of gays to their success.

Second, you are asking Ford to discriminate. Gays would be asking a company *not* to discriminate. Which is the fairer argument?

Eli: What does that mean—fair? The Bible says what is right, not what is fair. God is the only definer of right, of wrong, or even of fair. Obedience is what is expected.

Jay: I would have to say, "Whose God?" or "Whose interpretation of God are you saying everyone should obey?" You are expecting the whole world to follow what you and other fundamentalists believe to be true, even though a majority of the world's population is not a member of your conservative religion. That is the singular point. You are commanding people to believe, or at least obey, the religion you believe. Gays are asking people to look at the facts and give up prejudices society and sciences know are not true today. Even the mainstream, Christian believers in the United States would not side with your judgment of God's judgment.

Your statement about being fair is odd to me. Man defines fair as being what is right in a given situation according to commonsense mores. So, fair would be right. The Bible tells us to do the right, live uprightly, do justly, and love your neighbor as yourself—to be fair, in other words. Now you say simply to do what the Bible (and thus, according to you, God) says to do. "Obedience is what is expected." We are expected to do all things right, and thus obey God, but not every situation is covered in the mandates of the Bible. Therefore, it seems logical that we are to think and do that which we determine to be the right. Fair is the right then, and we are to obey. I am at a bit of a loss.

Similarly, what part of the Bible do we obey? How does the Bible define *right*? At one point, it is to love one another, to forgive, to advocate righteousness. But what is righteousness? Love and justice, I would assume. So, which justice do we support—the justice of health care for all equally, or the ignorance of the spirit of the law in favor of the letter of the law?

Further subtleties exist in the substance of what the company was asking for. In the case of health care and equal benefits for all, I would have to say that denying care to anyone, including criminals, would be an un-Christian thing to do. But, then, I see health care as a basic right for all mankind, not just for a privileged few. However, that is really a different question. In essence, we are arguing about which "right" is the strongest: the right of a personal belief system to influence other's decisions, about equal rights even, or the right of equal treatment and/or pay for equal work. Thus,

I do not agree with this argument you make that gays, with their boycotts, do essentially the same thing as Christians did in the Ford case. Demonstrating—or even boycotting, if it came to it—for the benefit of people seems to me to be acceptable, whereas boycotting to deny people a good is not acceptable.

Now, I have a simple question for you. Can you explain why your belief that the earth is young, only six thousand years old or so, and that God created the universe in six twenty-four hour days so important? Why is it so necessary to place a concrete interpretation on the creation story?

Eli: Because the Bible says six thousand years—or, just before Adam was made. Elohim did it in six days and rested the seventh. What other story is there? Who else was there?

Jay: The Bible does not say six thousand years. A man counted the years using the genealogies given in the Bible (like in Numbers) and came to that number. But the Hebrews used "father," "grandfather," and other terms interchangeably at times, sometimes skipping generations—rather like naming Abraham as the *father* of multitudes. But you know that.

I would assume that there is some set fundamentalist teaching about the differing versions of creation in the Y and P documents, and about the early chapters of Genesis?[4] I have no trouble with the creation point of Eve, when she was created out of Adam, but this variation of the same tale seems to demonstrate that the intricate

---

4   Though the book of Genesis is ostensibly authored by Moses, being the first of the five books of Moses, scholars do not agree with this. Further, nearly half a millennia appears to have occurred between parts of the writings. Three distinct styles in the book are recognized by some. The Y and E documents are based on the Hebrew word for God employed by the writer: Yahweh, or Elohim. The P document is more formal, and potentially penned by a priestly writer. You can find some analysis of this here: http://www.enotes.com/classical-medieval-criticism/genesis.

detail of the creation story is not the important point in the myth, just like the number of generations in other stories—father or great grandfather, et cetera. Interestingly, the second version has Eve created after God gives the order not to eat of the two trees. But she knows of the command when speaking with the serpent. Does this mean that God intends to tell only men the rules and women should learn from men, as Paul suggests sometimes? These details seem to me to be of little import. In a myth, it is the overall story that serves the purpose, too.

Eli: Have you heard or read of the gold chains, goblets, and candlesticks found in coal? Yes. Man-made, in a two-hundred-foot-thick seam of coal! Flood of Noah, anyone?

Jay: I have heard similar. First, there are many stories, myths, and records of massive floods. They happened. Covering the whole earth, over the highest mountain? I don't think so. I recall some scientist actually did some calculations, and simple mathematics determined that even with the melting of all the ice, there would not be enough water on the planet to flood the earth as completely as in the Noah story. Though, as a matter of intellectual curiosity, I do not know and do wonder whether the calculations included the water in the clouds.

Second, even I know geologically that at times, the land mass folds back over itself, which creates rather strange phenomenon. Nevertheless, this would be a question for a geologist. Have you bothered to ask one who actually studies this? Just go on a website for a university, find the geology department, and e-mail an instructor. Find a Christian one, even. Do not go to BYU or Jerry Falwell's university, as they do not deal with facts in the same way (so sorry— they simply are not credible sources for me).

If a school does not consider alternative views and approach them objectively to prove or disprove them, that school is not credible. If your schools, for example, just presented what you already believed, what did you learn? Did you already understand as an adult even when you were a child? Tell me, just how have you grown in understanding of God from childhood to adulthood?

Eli: I once wondered about the dinosaurs found in the book of Job—the account of the critter that has legs like tree trunks, living at the time of Job. Yep. Was it a myth or a real critter? Was it perhaps called a dragon in old England? I like the Bible. It has been here a long time. I like it better than the nursery rhymes … millions of years ago, there lived dinosaurs! In the Congo, natives there say they see what they describe as the same. Now, why not believe the Bible?

Jay: Well, the dinosaur skeletons we have found do not look at all like dragons, though there are the dragons (living on Sumatra I think). They could pass as dragons, at any rate, and they even have saliva, I read, that is acidic. We could take that as metaphorical fire, though I am not at all sure of this. Elephants also have treelike legs, we know, and that would have been in Job's area, possibly. Job, by the way, is another piece of literature not understood as actually happening but as a way of dealing with the question of the existence of evil in the universe of a good deity. As such, the book of Job does a good job of illuminating that question. Just threw that in, in case you were getting bored.

Eli: If I don't believe the non-myth of the first Adam, why should I believe the redemption story of the second and last Adam? Jesus quoted the Genesis story as if it were true; it really happened, snake and all. I doubt I have all the facts in line about all of it, but I think that story is as good as the one we evolved from a rock! I like the God thing better.

Jay: I never heard we evolved from a rock, but we are made of exploded stars. Anyway, the first and last Adam is one of my favorite images, but what do you mean the Bible has been here a long time? The King James Version is from King James's time, the 1600s—only around three hundred years ago. And the earliest Christian writing is either 1 Thessalonians or Galatians from about 49 CE. Even the Old Testament is not as old as the *Epic of Gilgamesh*, King of Uruk. We should also note that much of the mythology of the Hebrews comes from the area of Ur as well, as does Abraham, who came out from Ur of the Chaldees.

It seems you are saying you haven't grown, then? What do you believe now that you didn't as a teenager or even a preteen, and vice versa?

Eli: Oh, my growth is good. I have learned a lot about health and psychology, the mind and mental processes, deceiving and being deceived, people who love and ones who would like to love and be loved.

I have learned that Job is correct; life is full of things that we don't like. It is better to die than to live ... but the living is the source of knowing why! And I want to know why ... about a million things. I have learned that the Bible uses a lot of simile, metaphor, and symbols in its linguistics. One thing is like another, whether thing or person. I have learned God is truly slow to anger and slow to punish; he desires for all to come to repentance and is not willing that any die.

I could go on and on; the list is large. I think it wonderful that, as a person becomes old enough to have learned some smarts, he dies, and a young fool is born. When a young couple reproduces and finally learns to rear children, they then have aged a bit; they cannot have any more, and as grandparents, they aid the young, who do not know how to rear the next generation. God does things backward ... a lot of things. This I think until I see more.

These Lutheran and Episcopal bishops today are trying to rewrite the Bible—taking on themselves, or trying to take on, the power that was given to the original writers.

Jay: I think you sincerely and deeply believe as you do. You have not yet been able to understand what I am saying, though, my friend, nor really what the bishops are saying.

The bishops are not at all saying they have had a "new revelation" or that God has told them anything new. They are saying that through the passage of time and studying and experimentation and observation, we are all learning and understanding more about ourselves and our universe. As we understand more about disease, we too can heal and even prevent disease. As we learn more about our solar system, we can observe and explain phenomena that were at one time unexplainable, and at the same time find new phenomena that are even more awesome. As we learn more from archeology and history and language and cultures and psychology and sociology and religion, we can understand more in man's incessant search for meaning to his existence.

As we perceive man as a storyteller, we can see how the gift of words has enabled the metaphor of life to be expressed and the ability of finite minds to at least perceive the existence of the infinite— that which we call God. We can observe the development of this inexpressible concept from the simple, physical gods of the ancients (sun, moon, weather, battle, and village) into the philosophical and monotheistic concepts we are familiar with today. In my personal philosophy or theology (only mine), I rely on the numerous myths of the past of the dying gods and the resurrecting gods as the foreshadowing of the one true myth of the Christ. This story of ultimate truth did not just take place in time; it is somehow eternal.

Man is a capable creation. His mind is not an enemy of truth, and neither is God. The seeking of truth through education is not an evil. Education does not seek to destroy religion, but it will inevitably cut down the supports of a belief held up with mistaken foundations.

But that does not destroy faith or belief in truth. It only leads one to a truer understanding of God. We—the bishops and I and the liberals and the others who fight against this "proud bigotry" —do not say that God has changed his mind about homosexuality or right and wrong, but that man has not understood what God sees as right and wrong, because man looks through the paradigms of his own age and through the understandings of his own times and prejudices. The Bible may be the Word of God, but it is not the words of God, is how the saying goes, I believe.

Remember what I mentioned earlier, that astronomical event recently—that extraordinary happenstance? The one telescope focused on a particular part of a distant galaxy to observe a supernova that had been going for some time captured an anomaly. When the astronomer noticed the odd x-ray emanation from a neighboring star, she told other astronomers worldwide, and many of them focused their telescopes on the object.

That x-ray emanation turned out to be a second supernova just starting in the same galaxy. The interesting thing is that what they were watching was the light that had traveled around eighty-six million years to reach the telescope.

With all the research in agreement that the earth is not a mere six thousand years old—even the Vatican accedes to this—why is it necessary to hold on to the young-earth theories? What do they have to do with God? If we continue to deny truths discovered about our world and universe that contradict early understandings of religions, soon people will simply dismiss these religions and their gods as ludicrous and totally irrelevant to life and death. Even Saint Augustine saw this in his time, sixteen hundred years ago. Thus, the truths of God will go undiscovered, and much of the beauty and power of the universe that could be available to man will be ignored.

Jesus said even greater things will his followers do than he, as he goes to be with the Father. He fought against the bigotry of the

Pharisees and Sadducees—the self-righteousness that had replaced the true charity and love of God.

You know people who actually prayed for God to punish a business, Ford, for breaking a rule mentioned only very briefly in a huge book, and were willing to let thousands of believers and nonbelievers suffer economically just to show that your will needed to be done. Jesus did not destroy the temple; he drove out the sinners. Your friends prayed for God to rain down destruction on the temple of sin (Ford) and maim all those within the temple as well, figuratively speaking.

You do not affirm all I say and do, but I still would not pray for your destruction, just that you would see that, metaphorically, what you understood as a child and spoke as a child can change, and you could see as a man and speak as a man with new eyes and new understandings now. Understandings can and do change.

Eli: Now, what do you think Paul was saying when he said that all things are lawful for him, but not all things are expedient—pork, meat, fornication, adultery, stealing, hating without reason?[liii] *Leviticus 11 is adjusted a bit by the incident with Peter and the sheet—the parable, if you will, of the Old Testament Levites. When Peter saw the vision of the sheet and unclean animals, a truth was illuminated for him that what God had cleansed—meaning the gentiles—was not to be called unclean again.*[liv]

If a man says "I am a homosexual; God made me that way, and I am to practice sex with one other man, or many," knowing God has condemned the act, it is no different than a man saying that he is in love with another's wife, and God has made him that way, and therefore God wants him to pursue the lady. We still call that adultery, and it is to be warred against. The Old Testament says that adulterers are to be stoned. Today, at least the man should not see the other man's wife, and he should abstain from temptation and envisioning the sin. Sin is simply missing the mark of Christ's character—coming short of the image and glory of God.

Our task, as followers of Christ, is to press for the mark of the high calling in Christ Jesus, not make excuses for the temptations and opportunities for sin to be "normalized." God is the example, not the practitioners of the less than normal and godly lifestyle.

For me to say, "I lie at times; therefore it is normal and okay to lie," I think you would agree, would represent neither the image nor desire of Christ. Would you? So, if the whole world says that homosexuality or the lesbian lifestyle is the intent of God for some, and that all must accept it, it puts my thinking in the same minority as that of Noah when the whole world was given over to violence, and God said enough. So, only eight were saved from the flood. No myth, just a very big flood. It happened.

Can you make this clear? If I am forgiven all sin, is it okay to do what is sin to God?

Jay: I am not sure how to interpret "okay" in your context. Sin is not okay, or we would not always strive to do better. Jesus said to be perfect, but I only know of you and I who are perfect out of the entire world ... and sometimes I wonder about you. I don't mean to be flippant, but in other words, none have succeeded in perfection, so we have already, and always will, fail to reach the mark, which is an absence of sin, as you say.

Sin, in its most heinous forms, causes the evils of war, starvation, disease, poverty, fear, depression, greed, judgmentalism, tyranny, and oppression. So, I would have to say that sin is not okay in that sense. Some sin is based in selfishness or pride and is destructive. I tend to see the destructive as evil and the constructive as good. That is as close as I can come to relating to a definition of evil. Sin is a human condition; we always miss the mark, even Paul. I'm not sure what being forgiven has to do with making sin okay. I certainly am not saying that since one is forgiven, one's sins are to be disregarded. I'm saying we disagree on what particular actions are correctly understood as sinful.

We need to also consider, though, another part of the Bible. All things may be legal for Paul, he says, but not all things are expedient … and, again, if our heart condemns us, there is one greater than our heart. I think these references have a lot more resonance with God than most all of the condemning verses. The Bible gives little space to the murderers and adulterers and thieves compared to the space given to eternal truths of God's relation to mankind.

The Bible is not a book of lists of sins. Leviticus comes close, I grant you, but we do not seem to be too disturbed about breaking many of those laws today—like eating shellfish, and wearing mixed cloth, and even eating pork. Even Jesus said that the priests make the so-called righteous life so onerous that no one could live it. Listening to him, we might be better off proclaiming the Good News, not the bad.

Finally, if God *forgives* one for all sin, that indicates that sin is *not* okay to God, doesn't it? I mean, why would he need to forgive sin if it were okay? The statement isn't logical.

Anyway, I do not believe that sin is okay, nor do I believe it is the theme of the Bible. We proved unable to stop sinning once we started eating fruit, so God had to fix it himself. Now, how much time should we spend telling people not to sin compared with telling them that God fixed it?

So, when one preaches hellfire-and-brimstone sermons to sinners, is it to make them feel guilty, so they can accept the sacrifice? Could it be possible that there are enough beautiful and awesome things about God to draw people to him out of love and not just out of fear?

Eli: Forgiveness says he wants our company. Love says we want to do what is pleasing to him.

And we are to be salt in the world that will make the world like heaven on earth. Recall the Lord's Prayer: "… done on earth as it is in heaven."

Jay: As a side note, I find this "heaven on earth" statement to be fascinating. When evangelicals have criticized those they call the secular humanists for denying God or leaving him out of the equation, one of their strongest complaints has been that man wanted to make the world the way it should be when it is only God who can do that in the next world—at least that was my understanding of the complaint. But you seem to be saying that you will make heaven on earth now. That would be nice, but my reservations will come later.

Eli: My task is to preach Christ and push forcefully for his kingdom to be clearly seen on this planet—as his will is done in heaven. What do you think?

Jay: Honestly, it frightens me. Let me explain why. You want to push forcefully for his kingdom, and you assume that you know what that kingdom would and should be like. Now maybe you do, but maybe you do not. I think you would, in the extreme, be happy to force people at gunpoint to obey the laws of God as you see them. No other interpretation would be acceptable than yours or your religion's. How do you know that the part of God you know is the only part of God that exists?

I am willing to accept that you may see truths about God that I do not see, but I do not feel for a moment that you believe I or anyone else who does not agree with you on everything knows some part of God that you do not know. I do not mean this to be hurtful or mean, my friend, but you have not been able to even hear what I have to say about things I know about that you do not.

For example, you still are relating homosexuals to murderers and adulterers and baby rapists. You have not been able to grasp that what a person is, is different from what a person does. This drivel about the church accepting gays as long as they do not do anything gay is insane.

A thief goes out to take what is not his own, as does a murderer. The action of stealing defines a thief or a murderer; a homosexual only admits what is the self. Sexuality is perhaps the most definitive trait or characteristic of any given human being. It motivates marvelous creations and actions as well as the most dastardly deeds. It occupies the thoughts of men and women constantly. Paul admits its power when he says it is better to marry than to burn.[iv] God admits it when he says it is not good for man to be alone and makes a helpmate for him.

It is not something that one can simply deny. You are putting onto a percentage of the human race a burden you have not put on yourself (unless you are gay and have truly taken the route of self-sacrifice in marrying, but you told me you aren't, and I believe you).

Now, you will have a huge problem with this part, but you know it already, I think. I do not think that sin is the way to go. It is not profitable, and it hurts others as well as oneself. I am saying that it seems to be antithetical to the nature of God to believe what the Bible seems to say about homosexuality. I am saying I do not believe that homosexuality—or loving spiritually, emotionally, and physically—is the sin it is believed to be by conservative evangelicals.

I believe that men trying their best to interpret God and his will—according to the knowledge they had at the time—wrote the statements about homosexuality found in the Bible. I do not believe God made gays to be abominations to him. I do not believe God made thieves and murderers, but men may certainly become that if they steal or kill. Men do not become homosexuals because of their actions.

I should interject here that I do accept that some childhood abuse or incidents in a person's life can affect his or her behavior in negative as well as positive ways, though. A child molested certainly can become an adult with behavioral and psychological problems. That psychological damage is not the homosexuality I speak of, and I am not expert enough to discuss it. It is a different subject entirely.

I believe that we are in the middle of a major change in the world's understanding of sexuality and in the world's understanding of God. Just as the Catholic Church recently changed the centuries-old belief that limbo was the realm of un-baptized babies, the changing knowledge of God's creation will bring added knowledge of him. I do not see this as un-Christian or sinful.

Eli: What do you think of this? Take a listen. Writing about his visit to America in the early 1800s, Alexis de Tocqueville said,

> *I sought for the key to the greatness and genius of America in her harbors ... in her fertile fields and boundless forests; in her rich mines and vast world commerce; in her public school system and institutions of learning. I sought for it in her democratic Congress and matchless Constitution. Not until I went into the churches of America and heard her pulpits aflame with righteousness did I understand the secret of her genius and power. America is great because America is good, and if America ever ceases to be good America will cease to be great.*[lvi]

What does the "good" mean in that quote? Is it as defined in the Bible— since it referenced preaching in the churches?

Jay: When we try to put meaning to others' words, especially those of a different time period, we always must be wary. Nevertheless,

I think the writer, whoever it was (though it was not Alexis de Tocqueville), was referring to a moral good. We do call people good, so I suppose it could apply to countries as well, even though the Lord says there are none good except God.[lvii]

We allow people to use the term anyway. Interesting that this prophecy is again coming true, and America is losing her greatness as we are no longer good. I refer to the war and torture and the corporatocracy—the governing by huge corporations that forces developing countries into debt to the United States. They do this by loaning the countries money to hire huge corporations like Halliburton and Bechtel, et cetera, to build dams and other infrastructures. These projects really do nothing but enrich the top of the pyramid and bring the then-indebted country under the control of the United States. *Confessions of an Economic Hit Man* by John Perkins covers that issue very well.[lviii]

The quote you attribute to Alexis de Tocqueville is not found in any of his writings. There is a history of the quote beginning with Eisenhower and being enlarged by Reagan. Both used it for their own purposes, as you do now.[lix] You should be aware, though, that one of the main theses of Tocqueville was that the church must remain free from the government; for example, the government must not make laws about the way to interpret religion. As I recall, Tocqueville's *Democracy in America* continually echoes the themes that if religion joins with political powers, it will increase its power over some but lose out having power over all. He appears to believe that religions can nurture a moral life and that moral life then creates good citizens, which in turn creates a good country.[lx]

He did not sanction what we used to call legislating morality; rather, moral people (good, if you would) would naturally create moral republics. He adamantly opposed legislating methods of worship or even the necessity of worship or church. He objected to a historical law—in Connecticut, I think—that called for the death penalty for those who worshipped any other god but the one espoused by the rulers there or in any other manner than that dictated.

Our argument is not with whether the country, or even you or I, should be moral or good. We agree that we and the country should be. Rather, our search aims at discovering whether what we deem good might change as we discover more about human beings. We have changed ideas about women, slavery, food items, stoning children, and killing enemy babies and civilians, and we have grown in our understanding of demons possessing the ill. We see mental and physical health problems as being diseases that in many cases are treatable, like epilepsy and schizophrenia. We perceive witchcraft with different eyes today as well.

I think being "good" incorporates the ability to grow and change as understanding grows. God did not exist only in the first century, and what he did then is not what he does now. Remember Jesus saying that his followers would do even greater things than he did, as he was going to be with the Father? Part of doing greater things is most assuredly learning to use the insights we gain over the centuries and millennia to do not only good, but to do better, because we know more. We do not throw the lepers out to fend for themselves as their bodies fall apart; we treat them. We do not kill or imprison the insane because they have been possessed (though this unfortunately is debatable, given our current mental-health attitudes and treatments). At least we know better than to do that.

I offer another quote by Tocqueville: "The greatness of America lies not in being more enlightened than any other nation, but rather in her ability to repair her faults."[lxi] It is this repairing that I preach to America, to preachers and Christians, and to the world: repair the views of human sexuality to more correctly reflect contemporary knowledge.

Eli: Could trying to make America follow the good be a way of repairing? The Episcopalians have made a gay man a bishop. I think this is totally wrong, and so do many of the followers of that denomination. They can't seem to decide where they stand sometimes. The Bible holds the good right out in front of them: do this. All must choose the good.

The issue of homosexuality is dealt with clearly in the Bible. What was evil before the eyes of David in Psalm 101 is probably evil now. Looking on the nakedness of another man's wife, in spite of the bikini revolution, is probably still a lustful thing, as it was then for the king to look at the beautiful torso of the soldier's wife. David had the power. It was still wrong in the eyes of the Boss.

Jay: Yes. Trying to make America follow the good is definitely a way of repairing. I really do see you are trying to do this, and I applaud your purpose. Again, our differences develop around the source we use to determine the good. Within a complicated question, I try to include man's ability to reason; contemporary science and humanistic enlightenment; traditional practices; and the moral strictures that Christianity espouses to determine the right.

You, on the other hand, go a shorter route. Right, to you, seems to be the simple, verbatim statements from one book—much of it written prior to two thousand years ago. That book contains types of literature that do not lend themselves to verbatim interpretation. It also contains psychological and physiological errors that are totally understandable when we look at the level of knowledge available to the writers at that time. We no longer see slavery or stoning bad children to death as desirable. We no longer blame mental and physical diseases on demons.

The fundamentalist Christian fear of change or growth that contradicts the verbatim words of the Bible about slavery, foodstuffs, and disease has already shown itself to be baseless. Continuing to grow in understanding of the variables found in the Bible likewise will not necessarily undermine Christianity. However, denying truths that we understand through modern science and reason and that are clear today simply because they may contradict biblical statements written millennia ago will inevitably undermine any religion, including Christianity. How is one supposed to believe in a god that says the sun orbits the earth? Progress is not necessarily evil, but the fear of change is a potential evil.

Eli: Now be blunt. The desire of a man toward a woman sexually—his wife—is understood to amount to an undefiled marriage bed, in the general sense. This bishop who is "married" to his boyfriend—how does that work? What does this love look like? The passion for sex … is it kept to hugging and kissing, or is it more?

I heard of some ladies recently who were not a little angry at their husbands for doing more to them while they were asleep than the wives would allow even as a proposition to them while they were awake. They were not desirous of this type of lovemaking; they considered it to be like the sin of Sodom. I understand this to be common in the homosexual community. How does that work? I am just a student in these things.

Jay: Very well—I will be, as you say, "blunt." You asked earlier if gays keep the passion for sex to hugging and kissing in a homosexual marriage. Let me think about this. Do you keep the passion for sex to hugging and kissing in *your* marriage, or do other heterosexual husbands? Well, enough on that.

It seems physically unlikely that the husbands of these women you mention managed to "do more" while they were sleeping than when they were awake. However, do take note that heterosexuals also know and practice more things in the marriage bed than the missionary position, though you seem to be somewhat unaware of this.

Since you seem to be studying this phenomenon, I could say a few things about it. First, I have to admit I do not attempt to be an expert on sex, but I have friends who know more than I do. The argument taken by most literal biblical interpreters is that God made male and female, and they *fit* together, while two men do not. Well, of course male and female fit together. Preservation of the species demands it to some extent, doesn't it?

However, as the ladies you spoke of mentioned, sexual expression is not a matter of fitting in a particular way. The fit doesn't make it right or wrong, and if that were the only argument against gays—that they do not fit together—such an argument wouldn't hold water. You just mentioned, remember, that many heterosexuals fit together in the same way. Contrary to immediate reactions, sex isn't dirty at all, either. Showers, or baths, or even douches, are easily available. But, again, the manner in which one has sex really has nothing to do with love itself. Sex has to do with an expression, or an attempt to express, the longing to become one. I only answer your inquiry about this, since it is such an overused and mistaken argument put forth by the anti-gay forces.

Sex is a basic drive; nourishment—eating—is a basic need or drive. But we like variety in what we eat. Ice cream has very few positive benefits as far as nourishment is concerned. In fact we could live comfortably our whole lives and never once taste ice cream. It is merely a pleasure connected to the drive for nourishment, or the drive for life. So, sex is a need (made for reproducing the species and made to be enjoyable, so we will put up with the energy expenditure necessary), but we supply it with various interpretive actions.

Food is a basic need (made enjoyable for survival, or we wouldn't spend our lives working to get food); but again, we create or even interpret the various types of foodstuffs we choose to consume. Right and wrong are there as well, but they do not have to be confused with the concept of sex or eating. There are many reasons for the rules we have created for correct sexual and dietary behavior, and most of them are totally logical. Homosexual sex does not procreate. But then, neither does sex while the woman is pregnant or if one of the partners is infertile. It doesn't mean that they should stop sexual relations (unless, of course, one is Catholic).

The marriage bed provides a wonderful social and personal haven as well as the structure to grow and nourish a family. It is also a great way to pass on property and protect lineage that we think is important; just look at the Book of Numbers and the beginning of the gospel of Matthew. We need to prove that we are worthy. On the other hand, God is no respecter of persons.

If one takes the pope's dictate that sex is only for procreation, we had better get lust out of it altogether. Sex is ultimately enjoyable in order to further procreation. How the sex works—front, back, side, naked, clothed, underwater—is not directly connected to procreation, just enjoyment.

Straight people, especially conservative Christians, think only of the sex when gays seek recognition and rights. The gay existence is more like one seeking a helpmate, soul mate, and loved one of the same sex (though there are more than two genders plus gays, but for the sake of simplicity ...). Gay people are *not able* to experience that unity, that oneness with one of the opposite sex. They require emotional fulfillment through homosexual relations. There is a "cart before the horse" problem here.

Straights assume that sex drives homosexuality, but it does not drive them any more than it drives heterosexuals. Now, I know that we all have the drive, but we also recognize—some sooner than others, and some never—that the physical is not the real relationship any of us desire. It is an expression of what we desire but will never really have, perhaps, 'til we receive the answer to Jesus's prayer that we be one as he and the Father are one.

When you deny me or another person the ability to have a relationship like the one you have with your wife, you are saying you are okay to experience unity with another, but others are not. We must simply live life alone, always wanting but never having the helpmate that even God said we need when he said it is not good for man to be alone. To reverse my argument, as it is difficult to understand from the outside, you might say something like this:

You desire a wonderful blonde girl to marry and with whom to share your life, joys, sorrows, and family. However, in this hypothetical world, God says you cannot marry or love a girl; you must go against everything you feel and know and desire, and marry a man (who may be blonde, if you desire). There will be sex between the two of you, but it will not be what you desire, only your duty, because that is what God and society says you must do. Meanwhile, all those who feel and desire correctly in this imaginary world—that is, man for man and woman for woman—may have a mate and live with, and share with, and talk with, and care for one whom they desire. They get their desire; you don't, because they see your desire as wrong. What's more, they cannot understand what you see in girls anyway, so it shouldn't be hard for you. You must just do it ... period!

GOD VERSUS EDUCATION

Eli: All of that sounds very good, even intelligent, but let's look at intelligence or education in a different way. Listen to the story of this incident I read on the Internet. It is a bit long, but I will tell it as I remember it. Then, you can comment on it:

Did God create everything that exists? Does evil exist? Did God create evil? A university professor at a well-known institution of higher learning challenged his students with this question: "Did God create everything that exists?"

A student bravely replied, "Yes, he did!"

"God created everything?" the professor asked.

"Yes Sir, he certainly did," the student replied.

The professor answered, "If God created everything, then God created evil. And, since evil exists, according to the principle that our works define who we are, then we can assume God is evil."

The student became quiet and did not respond to the professor's hypothetical definition. The professor, quite pleased with himself, boasted to the students that he had proven once more that the Christian faith was a myth.

Another student raised his hand and said, "May I ask you a question, Professor?"

"*Of course,*" *replied the professor.*

The student stood up and asked, "Professor, does cold exist?"

"*What kind of question is this? Of course it exists. Have you never been cold?" The other students snickered at the young man's question.*

The young man replied, "In fact, Sir, cold does not exist. According to the laws of physics, what we consider cold is in reality the absence of heat. Every body or object is susceptible to study when it has or transmits energy, and heat is what makes a body or matter have or transmit energy. Absolute zero (-460F) is the total absence of heat, and all matter becomes inert and incapable of reaction at that temperature. Cold does not exist. We have created this word to describe how we feel if we have no heat."

The student continued, "Professor, does darkness exist?"

The professor responded, "Of course it does."

The student replied, "Once again you are wrong sir, darkness does not exist either. Darkness is in reality the absence of light. Light we can study, but not darkness. In fact, we can use Newton's prism to break white light into many colors and study the various wavelengths of each color. You cannot measure darkness. A simple ray of light can break into a world of darkness and illuminate it. How can you know how dark a certain space is? You measure the amount of light present. Isn't this correct? Darkness is a term used by man to describe what happens when there is no light present."

Finally the young man asked the professor, "Sir, does evil exist?"

Now uncertain, the professor responded, "Of course, as I have already said. We see it every day. It is in the daily examples of man's inhumanity to man. It is in the multitude of crime and violence everywhere in the world. These manifestations are nothing else but evil.

To this the student replied, "Evil does not exist, Sir, or at least it does not exist unto itself. Evil is simply the absence of God. It is just like darkness and cold, a word that man has created to describe the absence of God. God did not create evil. Evil is the result of what happens when man does not have God's love present in his heart. It's like the cold that comes when there is no heat, or the darkness that comes when there is no light."

The professor sat down.

The young man's name—Albert Einstein—a true story.

Well? What do you think of that story?

Jay: First, it is not a true story, as it asserts. It is an interesting anecdote. However, that narrative contains so many faults, I am not sure where to start. Certainly it was not Einstein or anyone with an education in logic, though. Many discuss the tale as an urban legend on the same Internet where it came from.[lxii] Notice that, in the definition of evil, the student uses God's existence to prove that God exists. That is classic circular reasoning. Besides, Einstein quit believing in that type of universe or God at the age of twelve.

Some other points are also important to that story, however.

First: I have always heard one should not try to prove a negative—for example, "God does not exist," as the professor seems to attempt to prove. Anyway, God is not in the proof arena.

Second: Isaiah 45 tells us of God telling Cyrus that he, God, creates evil and darkness.

Third: The concept that a man's works define who he is is an existential philosophical premise. Consider, for example, two men. Gandhi defined man and Hitler defined man through their works. Thus, man is both capable of good, self-sacrifice, and love, as well as capable of horrendous destruction. The application of this reasoning to God, as in "he created evil; therefore he is evil," is not correct. The work of God was the *creating*, not what he created. Thus, and rightly, we can define God as a creator. He supposedly created fish as well, didn't he? Does that make him a fish?

The real problem with this argument is that too many people in the fundamental and conservative churches believe what the writer of this story believes: the philosophy professor is a bad person, an atheist, who is trying to destroy the faith of the innocent. While this is sometimes the case, this simplistic story does not do what it ought to do; it just prejudices the reader against all the stuff he does not know or understand. It makes, by extension, education an evil and a danger, and, my friend, I suspect you think that is true.

Fourth: The important point of this anecdote lies in the truth it could present—that evil *is* the perversion of the good, and that darkness is the absence of the light. Even though, according to Isaiah, God did create both, they are derivatives of the other.

If one thinks of sins individually, like gluttony, stealing, drunkenness, lasciviousness, and so on, they are all derivatives of a good and could not exist if the good were not there first.

Eating is good; food is good. It is only when eating is perverted and becomes obsession that it exhibits evil. For example, gluttony is not just eating too much; according to C. S. Lewis, even requesting only a dry piece of toast when you are a guest at a dinner can be gluttony as well. It is a perversion of the good, because it insists that *to meet your specific desires*, the hostess must redo the dinner menu. That makes food a potential evil. Property, or acquiring property, or even objects, is good, as they are necessary for existence. Only when one takes or lusts after what is not his own does it become perverted and thus an evil.

Drink is given to gladden the heart of man (and it does, if you have never been gladdened), but the overuse of it (I do not mean alcoholism; that is a disease) is how it can become evil. Alcohol can be misused to justify actions of which we do not approve, to seek oblivion when we need to face up to something, to live a life of "party hearty" instead of a life that benefits others and the self.

Sex is good too, as we know; only when it is perverted to hurt others or to become the idol of our existence does it assume evil traits. When it becomes the obsession that causes us to neglect the rest of our lives, or hurts others, or (in the case of the church) when the obsession with sexual sin becomes the "sexy" focus to lead members to where the church wants them to be (in the United States on the Republican ticket), does it become evil. And, to answer your interjection I can hear coming, my case is that homosexuality is not the perversion of a good, as is assumed by most. It is a norm, a natural part of the human and animal species. (I haven't considered fish at this point.)

But sexual sin is an evil just like all other evils. It hurts man in that it hinders him in being all he can be; he misses the mark for one reason or another. Our argument on homosexuality hinges here. You think something is a perversion based on a few biblical references from a time that could not understand the varieties of man. I do not see it as a perversion, based on current, scientific research, commonsense observations, logical reasoning, and my personal knowledge of God.

I do not deny the Bible says what it does, but it also says the sun stopped.[lxiii] I do not even care if it happened or not; we know the sun would not have stopped, but stopping the earth's rotation would create that illusion. Does this new understanding hurt the story? No. We do not need to seek extraordinary means to figure out why the text presents the exact events that it does; the story makes its point anyway.

Fifth: You distress me by the use of the word "myth" in "… that religious faith was a myth." We should consider a couple of points here, my friend. Religious faith exists; it is not a myth. The professor was really saying faith is illogical or that God doesn't exist. It is difficult to argue if the language isn't accurate.

We often refer to something untrue as a myth. That is one of the definitions of the word. My fear here is that you will see it as the word I use when I say the Garden of Eden story is a myth or Noah's story is mythic. In these references, I am not using the definition of untrue, I am using the literary definition of a type of literature, usually referencing the gods or the supernatural used to demonstrate and preserve a *truth* of the people who hold that myth in their mythos. (Mythos is the collection of beliefs that distinguish a people and make them a unique group in history.) Understanding this is the key to understanding this argument.

Sixth: The student's response that cold and darkness and evil do not exist because he says physics defines them as the absence of something is not a very convincing argument, as he is offering the definition of them in his statement, and that, by implication, says they exist as recognizable properties. Further, they do exist, as does hunger, the absence of nourishment, death, the absence of life, and so on.

Many of these professors are the way they are because certain types of Christians have deeply wounded them in the past. They also see the fruits of religious fanaticism and, illogically, transfer that violence and bigotry to God. What that professor may need, perhaps, is interaction with Christians who carry the Good News, and its love and joy—Christians who see through the suit of armor of these people, considered to be atheistic and mean, to the hurting soul underneath. Someday, God will show us the beauty of the worst among us and help us to understand his love for them. At that point, perhaps mankind will be one, as Jesus and the Father are one—when we can drop the lenses of judgment, when the beam is finally removed from our eyes, and when we can see to reach out to the drunkards, the adulterers, the fanatics, and even the murderers as wounded brothers and sisters.

Finally, it is for the above reasons I must strongly and sincerely disagree with the heading of that story: "this is good." It isn't good, I'm sorry. It only comforts or makes one feel superior because the kid appeared to exact revenge on the professor. Vengeance is not good. Also, the logic is not sound. It contributes to the error of assuming that educated people are evil, and even the child can outsmart them. I fear this story has caused and will cause more hard feelings on the one side and more wrong thinking on the other. Therefore: not good. Sorry, nothing personal.

Afterword

Predictably, when I tell people the title of this book, their first question is, "Who won?" The answer to this does not have to be one side or the other. In a meaningful argument, all parties could be winners. If a subject is arguable, there must be truths present on all sides, or there would be nothing to argue. If only one side had any truth, facts would present the obvious solution. Debating which building is the highest would be useless; simply measure the buildings. Facts settle the debate. Likewise, a matter of taste doesn't make a good argument. One prefers vanilla, the other prefers strawberry. That is not fuel for a quarrel. A real argument, one of value, can discover truths—if not ultimate truth, at least greater truth. The journey, the trip itself, becomes part of the destination. We should see many new truths, perspectives, challenges even, as we travel through the landscape of ideas. Most animals use their brains for concrete answers, but only man employs the brain for complex, intangible problems. Using reason to find truths differentiates man from other creatures, and reason is definitely required in arguing the complex issues involved in the gay question.

Clearly, the actual argument in this book is not the surface argument of whether gays are going against God's laws or purpose. It is rather, "What is God's law or purpose?" And the dividing issue is the mechanism for discovering the right. The fundamentalist deems the debate to be of little consequence, because whatever the Bible says (to him, what God says) is the final word on all subjects. The opposing view that God is not simply a finite being or concept, but rather he and his laws transcend the human definitions found in sacred writings, does not alter that the proponents of both views are seeking the right. To find this right, men and women must examine any god and any hallowed writing under the microscope of reason. If one truly believes that a deity created man in the image of a god, then reason is part of that image, and one is required to employ the brain and thought as readily as any of the senses or other attributes.

I have attempted in this dialogue to limit the discussion of sexuality to heterosexuality and homosexuality. Other orientations or proclivities are for another to explore. Further, just because the dialogue makes a case for the rational deliberation of homosexuality, it is not a plea to throw aside all morality or judgment. I can think of no one who would unquestioningly advocate all of the practices in the gay community. While it is true that gays have an earned reputation for excess in public sexuality, with nudity, promiscuity, even drug and alcohol abuse readily in evidence, these also flourish in the straight community. Gays did not invent these practices, nor can we single gays out for criticism because of them.

This singling-out phenomenon is extremely dangerous and deceitful when appraising the complexities of human behavior. The rising conservatism and evangelicalism of much of Africa referred to in *Arguing with God* is a breeding ground for these activities and can serve as an example. Uganda is considering legislation that has brought almost universal condemnation by the civilized world. That legislation would call for criminal punishment for being gay, or not turning in one known to be gay. The penalties can include execution.[lxiv]

The proponents of this anti-gay legislation have singled out a particularly distasteful sexual practice of a small number of homosexuals (as well as heterosexuals, though that is not mentioned). One speaker who is denouncing the gays uses this specific practice to define what homosexuality is and what all homosexuals do. Having extended this accusation to include all gays, the advocates of this misinformation then preach that homosexuals will entice and victimize schoolchildren, forcing them to participate in this marginalized sexual practice, or even recruit the children into becoming homosexuals. This is one way the mistaken belief that people choose their sexual orientation becomes a weapon in the hands of homophobes. These are truly homophobic examples, as evidenced by their use of fear tactics to elicit hatred, and inevitably violence, against gays.

These proponents call these outrageous charges the homosexual agenda. If that were true, it would be an absurd and unprofitable agenda. Do heterosexuals recruit children into heterosexuality? The only sexual recruitment of which I am aware is that of the religious institutions who falsely claim they can change a gay's orientation to straight. It doesn't work. Gays, at least, are aware of this and do not recruit. Please note that I am not discussing pedophiles. That is an entirely different subject, and, statistically, most pedophiles are heterosexual anyway.

One who seeks the truth may not include these or similar conspiracy theories and emotional appeals in a rational quest for truth and right. Neither heterosexuality nor homosexuality is the same thing as pedophilia, and pedophilia has no inherent connection to any other specific sexual practice. Further, illogical and closed-minded attacks keep adversaries debating only the shell of the argument instead of conducting a more profitable exploration of deeper elements within the gay question that they could be considering.

Similarly, focusing on only the emotionally packed themes tends to keep the other issues invisible. Neither accepting gays as one of God's creations—meant to live life to the fullest, just as the straight man or woman—nor accepting the legality of gay marriage answers the whole of the question. For example, the fundamentalists readily condemn the loose, hedonistic behavior of gays. They decry their lack of monogamy and strict moral standards. Of course, denying marriage to gays certainly does not encourage monogamous behavior, either, but this undisciplined behavior might be worth a second look.

Could it be that religion again plays a key role in this apparent hedonism? Certainly religion is not the ground of this hedonism, but could it be contributory? This does not mean that I am placing the blame for the excesses of anyone solely on religion. We need to realize, though, that there is no cause to try to observe the delicacies of modesty or chastity when Christian society has already labeled one as unacceptable, an outcast, and an abomination. If the horses are already out of the barn, why bother to lock the doors? If one's whole nature makes one a pariah and an exile outside the definition of morality to the club, why follow any of the rules of the club? The faith community appears to unintentionally nurture the promiscuity it criticizes so loudly.

Likewise, these conservative Christians appear to be wearing a type of blinder. It is probably understandable. Observed from the outside, it is easy to assume all gays fit the mold seen in gay parades, or seedy movies, or other staged venues. But, as are most performance images, these figures are larger than life. Nevertheless, just as with the straight society, individuals in the gay society differ greatly in their interpretation of ethics, morality, and spirituality. The gay community also encompasses couples who have lived together for fifty years or more in monogamous relationships. Their love for one another is strong enough to see them through decades of ostracism and misunderstanding, and their contribution to a moral society should be unquestioned. Many others have parented children—either adopted, or brought from an earlier heterosexual marriage, or conceived through a surrogate or other medical techniques. Hundreds of thousands of gay men and women exist, and the percentage of them searching for meaning, for truth, and even for God, equates the percentage of searchers in the straight community.

The vilification of a part of the human family, creating the outsider, the other, burns through our history from the hunter-gatherers to the inheritors of the nuclear bomb. Even the idea of the *family* of mankind seems to be merely wishful thinking. Religions should not be the inspiration for this prejudice, intolerance, and exclusion. Even the common man can look around him and see that homosexuality is neither a choice, nor a punishment from God. But he must look over the wall of condemnation to see this clearly. Could society lifting the blanket of moral condemnation of the gays encourage a standard, pragmatic morality of homosexuality to develop?

A quick review of the historical development of heterosexual mores in society shows a gradual movement through various coupling and sexual experiments. Now that marriage has finally mutated into what we acknowledge today—going through steps wherein women were bought and sold for money or power; polygamy was the norm in the highest places; the lower classes were not even granted the right to marry; and slaves were bred by Christian owners as cattle—we can discern a slow evolution in the definition of marriage. The family was not always the sweet, nuclear, or moral construct we pretend to have today. Mankind took millennia to define the current heterosexual borders, and they are neither uniform nor complete even now.

Likewise, homosexuality will be primed to evolve its own borders only after it is no longer in exile from the family of man, and gays can recognize they have need of their own boundaries. We can see this more clearly if we think of the fundamentalist's exaggeration of gays being equivalent to murderers or thieves. Thieves and murderers do not feel compelled to place limits on their treatment of victims, since they are already outside the law. If they are already outside the law, why make more laws? And we are not surprised when outlaws do not make great laws. Gays are a bit like orphans living outside the range of heterosexual mores. The heterosexual customs, likewise, do not quite fit the gay relationship, although many gay couples and singles do attempt to follow a morality developed in the straight world. They may be monogamous (or at least serially monogamous) even celibate, just as many heterosexuals are.

It is unlikely that all or any of this reasoning and argument will be included in most public discourse concerning homosexuality. Actually, most public discourse on the matter is merely a report of hostile actions or reactions (and what the media imparts is itself sometimes angry or biased reporting). Condemnations from one side charge the courts with judicial activism and legislating from the bench—some even voice outright accusations of attempted genocide or the destruction of society, should same-sex marriage be allowed. From the other side, we hear hurled epithets of bigotry, prejudice, ignorance, and closed-mindedness, at times painting all Christians, all faiths, and even God with the brush of hatred because of this bitter conflict. Society, government, and politics are now struggling with issues that divide not only the United States but the world. Still, many have not seen the battles in the stark terms of reason versus faith.

The argument between faith and reason was strong in the eighteenth Century; the Age of Reason supposedly supplanted the Age of Faith about the time the United States relied on the ideas of the Enlightenment to lay its foundations. Many assume that this war has ended, but the battles between faith and reason are bellowing from the front pages of newspapers and playing lead roles in television network news shows. Gay marriage, gay adoption, gay clergy, gay politicians, even the basis of homosexuality—is it merely a lifestyle choice or a permanent, inborn component of the human condition?—occupy the headlines. All of these are subjects of controversy within political parties and religious faiths, and the ensuing battles threaten the well-being of people and institutions on both sides of the issue.

Some fundamentalist faiths perceive a huge threat. The premise that God created gays is very telling, and those who believe that the Bible claims being gay is an abomination run into a bit of a wall here. If God does create some humans as gay, and it is not a choice, this leaves one with the truth that gays have a disadvantage. God supposedly created man and woman with an instinctual drive, one stronger in humans than any motivating drive other than self-preservation, and this drive answers the admonitions to love and to fill the earth with more humans. But if God creates some as gay (and we are not talking about birth defects or fallen man), this is an unfair playing field. Some are driven to play the game; others are driven to not play the game. Indeed, the playing field and the rules of the game do not make much sense at all. It is as if the creation story and the admonitions to go forth and populate the earth are elements of myth and do not really define the physiological and emotional condition of man. And, since to some fundamentalists, myths are just lies, Christianity itself is open to doubt.

The battle over the gay question is definitely under way. It is not simply a disagreement over sexual preference or orientation. It has morphed into a political issue. In an already polarized society, the issue is a wedge utilized to divide us further. Preachers and politicos in synchronous paths to win elections and to keep and gain power wield a hammer to drive the wedge between sides. Because it is an emotionally charged topic, it becomes a decisive issue in elections—coaxing out the normally apathetic voter. None of this, though, deals with the real victims, the wounded left behind on the battlefield. The hatred it evokes and the emotional level at which the arguments operate too often negate the objective thinking and even altruism that must be present to rightly govern a prosperous republic. Politicians run and often are elected solely on the basis of their adherence to one camp or the other rather than on their abilities or their understanding of a complex world. So, the gay question is not one affecting only gays and anti-gays, the evident participants. Instead, it encompasses the entire nation. It is a question that we all must answer, and we must answer with reason, not faith. Why? Reason is accessible to all men; a common faith is not.

Spiritual Tangents

The following works, while not dealing necessarily with the topic of sexuality in the church, offer a perspective on God and religions that may offer truths that fundamentalism does not often explore. They may prove enlightening to some who are seeking a way to God and self beyond the conservative, fundamentalist religions. The list is in no way comprehensive, of course, and I have not included all of the writings of C. S. Lewis, which I also recommend. The purpose of these selections is to offer an alternative to those who would simply reject religion, or Christianity, or even God when fundamentalists attack and alienate those who are different from themselves.

Armstrong, Karen. *The Battle for God*. New York: Alfred A. Knopf, 2000.

Borg, Marcus J., and John Dominic Crossan. *The Last Week: What the Gospels Really Teach About Jesus's Final Days in Jerusalem*. New York: HarperCollins, 2007.

Borg, Marcus J. *The God We Never Knew: Beyond Dogmatic Religion to a More Authentic Contemporary Faith*. New York: HarperCollins, 1997.

Bunch, Charles K., PhD. *The Wizard of Oz: The Symbolic Quest to Find Your Inner Heroes, Face Your Worst Enemy, and Attain Wholeness.* New York: iUniverse, 2006.

Capra, Fritjof, and David Steindl-Rast. *Belonging to the Universe: Explorations on the Frontiers of Science and Spirituality.* New York: HarperCollins, 1992.

Einstein, Albert, Carl Seelig, ed., and Sonja Bargmann, trans. *Ideas and Opinions.* Avenel, New Jersey: Random House, 1954.

Goldberg, Michelle. *Kingdom Coming: The Rise of Christian Nationalism.* New York: W. W. Norton and Company, 2006.

Houston, Jean. *A Mythic Life: Learning to Live Our Greater Story.* New York: HarperCollins, 1996.

Meacham, Jon. *American Gospel: God, the Founding Fathers, and the Making of a Nation.* New York: Random House, 2006.

Pagels, Elaine. *Adam, Eve, and the Serpent.* New York: Random House, 1989.

————. *Beyond Belief: The Secret Gospel of Thomas.* New York: Random House, 2004.

Primack, Joel R., and Nancy Ellen Abrams. *The View from the Center of the Universe: Discovering Our Extraordinary Place in the Cosmos.* New York: Penguin Group, 2006

Ricard, Matthieu, Trinh Xuan Thuan, and Ian Monk, trans. *The Quantum and the Lotus: A Journey to the Frontiers Where Science and Buddhism Meet.* New York: Random House, 2001.

Robinson, Gene. *In the Eye of the Storm: Swept to the Center by God.* New York: Seabury Books Church Publishing, 2008.

Rubenstein, Richard E. *When Jesus Became God: The Struggle to Define Christianity during the Last Days of Rome.* New York: Harcourt, 2000.

Spong, John Shelby. *Into the Whirlwind: The Future of the Church.* Haybridge, New Jersey: St. Johann Press, 2003.

———. *This Hebrew Lord: A Bishop's Search for the Authentic Jesus.* New York: HarperCollins, 1993.

———. *Why Christianity Must Change or Die: A Bishop Speaks to Believers in Exile.* New York: HarperCollins, 1998.

Wilber, Ken. *The Marriage of Sense and Soul: Integrating Science and Religion.* New York: Doubleday, 1998.

Zajonc, Arthur. *Catching the Light: The Entwined History of Light and Mind.* New York: Bantam Books, 1993.

Zukav, Gary. *The Dancing Wu Li Masters: An Overview of the New Physics.* New York: William Morrow and Company, 1979.

Video

Karslake, Daniel, director. *For the Bible Tells Me So.* DVD. New York: First Run Features, 2007.

NOTES

i.   See Romans 1:20 to the end of the chapter. Notice that though reference to what we may consider homosexual practice is evident, it is the punishment for substituting creature gods—idols—for the invisible God. This is like the gods modeled after man or animals. There are also descriptions of those punished *with* lusting (not *for*) after their same sex as becoming treacherous, murderers, undutiful to parents (not supportive), heartless, loveless, and merciless. I am not sure this describes accurately the homosexual community that is present today. They are mainly in families or couples, and many are even practicing Christians—not evil, jealous, and faithless murderers.

ii.   See 2 Peter 3:8 for this statement. Notice the larger picture: that the concept of time itself can be as fluid as the writer wishes.

iii.   See chapter 22 of both the gospels of Matthew and chapter 12 of Mark for this story.

iv.   See Genesis 2:18 for this statement by God.

v. See, again, Paul's letter to the Romans 7:19, but one needs to study the entire chapter to grasp that Paul is exploring the dichotomy of the physical, still-sinful self (which is theoretically dead, having been crucified with Christ) and the new nature, the "inner man" who hates sin, thus proving itself to be in agreement with Christ.

vi. See Michael Hampson, "A Loss of Faith," The *Guardian*, October 16, 2006, accessed December 10, 2010, http://www.guardian.co.uk/commentisfree/2006/oct/16/comment.religion.

vii. See 1 John 3:12 for John's statement that even when our hearts condemn us, God is greater than one's heart and knows all things: one of the beautiful concepts of God's unfailing love even for those who have been taught to despise themselves.

viii. See the gospel of John 13:35 for this saying of Jesus on his last night with his disciples.

ix. See Matthew 11:28.

x. See Acts 4:12.

xi. See Leviticus, chapter 21.

xii. See 1 Corinthians 10:13.

xiii. See Matthew 5:17.

xiv. See "Pat Robertson Controversies," accessed November 8, 2010, http://www.cbsnews.com/2300-503544_162-101.

html?tag=mncol;lst;2, for access to several of Robertson's statements linking disasters like Hurricane Katrina, the Haitian earthquake, and even terrorist attacks to sins of a nation. The idea of God intervening and punishing countries or cities for transgression was commonly accepted prior to the 1700s and is still extant today in many Islamic and Christian belief systems.

xv.   The gospel of John, chapter 14, presents Jesus saying that those who follow him will do greater things than he has done, because he must leave and go to the Father.

xvi.   See 1 Kings 19:12.

xvii.   See Numbers, chapter 22, for the story of Balaam and his ass.

xviii.   See Savitri Hensman, "The Anglican Power Play," *The Guardian*, June 30, 2010, accessed December 10, 2010, http://www.guardian.co.uk/world/belief/2010/jun/30/religion-anglican-covenant-homophobia for a synopsis of the Episcopal-Anglican unpleasantness.

xix.   See Angelica Martinez and Greg Gross, "Mistrial declared in firefighters' gay-pride parade suit," SignOnSanDiego.com, by *The Union Tribune*, October 6, 2008, last accessed December 10, 2010, http://legacy.signonsandiego.com/news/metro/20081006-1744-bn06parade2.html, and "News Outrage! Firefighters forced into 'gay' parade sue city," *WorldNetDaily*, August 28, 2007, last accessed December 10, 2010, http://www.wnd.com/index.php?fa=PAGE.view&pageId=43250, for coverage of this incident.

xx. See Eric Foner and John A. Garraty, eds., "Milestones in the Gay Rights Movement," excerpted from *The Reader's Companion to American History* (New York: Houghton Mifflin, 1991), at http://www.infoplease.com/ipa/A0194028.html#axzz0wFl2bPIs, last accessed December 10, 2010, for a thorough and easily accessible briefing on the history of gay rights.

xxi. See the Church of Ireland website, http://www.ireland.anglican.org/index.php?do=news&newsid=2029, last accessed December 10, 2010 (originally added July 22, 2007), for the sermon preached by the archbishop of Armagh, the Most Reverend Alan Harper, at Clonmacnoise.

xxii. See Genesis, chapter 11, for the story of the Tower of Babel and the confusion of men's languages.

xxiii. See Matthew, chapter 19, for Jesus speaking of Moses and divorce.

xxiv. See chapter 9 of the gospel of John for this story.

xxv. See Genesis, chapter 6, for the beginning of the Noah story.

xxvi. See Stephanie Dalley, ed., *Myths from Mesopotamia: Creation, the Flood, Gilgamesh, and Others* (New York: Oxford University Press, 2008) for good coverage of the Sumerian and Babylonian myths.

xxvii. See Genesis 18 for the beginning of the story of Sodom and Gomorrah. Often, the beginning of the story is ignored and should not be.

xxviii. See "GLAAD slams Sopranos star and pool cue company," *PageOneQ*, August 13, 2007, last accessed December 10, 2010, http://pageoneq.com/news/2007/GLAAD_slams_Sopranos_star_and_pool_cue_co_0814.html, for information regarding a pool cue named for an act of sodomy and murder on the television series *The Sopranos*. It was marketed by an Oregon company, but it has since been pulled off the market after many objections.

xxix. See all of chapter 2 of Mark to understand this statement of Jesus.

xxx. See J. Matt Barber, "Gays don't want marriage after all," *WorldNetDaily*, posted July 6, 2007, last accessed December 10, 2010, http://www.wnd.com/news/article.asp?ARTICLE_ID=56521, for the commentary "Gays' don't want 'marriage' after all."

xxxi. See Romans 3:23.

xxxii. See "Ted Baehr Tells International Religious, Political Leaders that Jesus Christ and God's Love, Not Tolerance, Is the Answer," *OpenHeaven.com*, May 1, 2005, last accessed December 10, 2010, http://www.openheaven.com/forums/forum_posts.asp?TID=15822.

xxxiii. See Bruce Schreiner, "Conservative Presbyterians Leave Church (PCUSA)," *FreeRepublic.com*, posted October 12, 2007, last accessed December 10, 2010, http://www.freerepublic.com/focus/f-religion/1910400/posts.

xxxiv. See Vernon J. Bourke, *The Essential Augustine* (Indianapolis, Indiana: Hackett Publishing Company, 1974), for the commentary and selected works of St. Augustine.

xxxv. See Stephanie Dalley, ed., *Myths from Mesopotamia: Creation, the Flood, Gilgamesh, and Others* (New York: Oxford University Press, 2008), for good coverage of the Sumerian and Babylonian myths. This being the geographical area from which the Patriarch Abraham hailed, there are many Mesopotamian myths that echo in the Jewish stories of the Old Testament as well.

xxxvi. See Genesis 2.

xxxvii. See 1 Corinthians 3:2.

xxxviii. See Acts, chapters 10 and 11.

xxxix. See Harold Meyerson, "God and His Gays," *The Washington Post*, March 21, 2007, A15. It can be found at *The Washington Post*'s website as well, last accessed December 10, 2010, http://www.washingtonpost.com/wp-dyn/content/article/2007/03/20/AR2007032001428.html.

xl. See Lynne Duke, "A Pre-Birth Determination?" *The Washington Post*, March 18, 2007, D1. It can also be read online at *The Washington Post*'s site, last accessed December 10, 2010, http://www.washingtonpost.com/wp-dyn/content/article/2007/03/17/AR2007031701162.html.

xli.   Bart D. Ehrman, *Misquoting Jesus: The Story Behind Who Changed the Bible and Why* (New York, New York: HarperCollins, 2005).

xlii.   Bruce Bagemihl, *Biological Exuberance: Animal Homosexuality and Natural Diversity* (London: Profile Books, 1999).

xliii. See Matthew 22 and Mark 12.

xliv.   See Matthew 5:17.

xlv.   See 1 Corinthians 8.

xlvi.   See Matthew 15:5 in the Revised Standard Version, as the King James is a bit obscure in its language here.

xlvii. See John 14:12.

xlviii. See the treatment of women and slaves, as well as the killing of women and children in the Israelite's battles in many places in the Pentateuch (the five books of Moses, first five books of Old Testament). Numbers 31 and Leviticus 25 offer some examples.

xlix.   C. S. Lewis, *God in the Dock: Essays on Theology and Ethics* (Grand Rapids, MI: Wm. B. Eerdmans Publishing Co., 1994).

l.   See Luke, chapter 10, for the parable of the Good Samaritan.

li.   See Matthew, chapter 6.

lii.   See Matthew, chapter 22, for Jesus's discussion of these as the first and second commandments and the notion that the entire law and prophets rest on these two: love God, and love your neighbor as yourself.

liii.   See 1 Corinthians 10:23. There is a little different intent from 6:12 of this book.

liv.   Acts 10 and 11 tell how God instructed Peter through a vision that what God has made clean, Peter should not call unclean.

lv.   See 1 Corinthians 7:9.

lvi.   This quotation repeats throughout the Internet, and its origin is unknown. Though attributed to Tocqueville, it is not his. This website gives a fair account of it, and this section of *Arguing with God* discusses it again. The website says, "Reverend John McDowell used the alleged quotation in a sermon on Labor Day weekend in September 1922 in New York City. It is not known where McDowell got the quotation from, but similar (though not exact) quotations have been found from 1886 and1908." See Barry Popik, "America is great because she is good," May 24, 2009, last accessed December 10, 2010, http://www.barrypopik.com/index.php/new_york_city/entry/america_is_great_because_she_is_good.

lvii.   See Mark 10:18.

lviii. John Perkins, *Confessions of an Economic Hit Man* (New York: Penguin Group, 2004).

166

lix.   See John J. Pitney Jr., "The Tocqueville Fraud," *The Weekly Standard*, November 13, 1995, last accessed December 10, 2010, http://www.tocqueville.org/pitney.htm.

lx.   See Alexis de Tocqueville, *Democracy in America*, 1805–1859, volumes 1 and 2, Electronic Text Center, University of Virginia Library, last accessed December 10, 2010, http://etext.lib.virginia.edu/toc/modeng/public/TocDem1.html and http://etext.lib.virginia.edu/toc/modeng/public/TocDem2.html.

lxi.   See Alexis de Tocqueville, *Democracy in America*, 1805–1859, volume 1, chapter 13, Electronic Text Center, University of Virginia Library, last accessed December 10, 2010, http://etext.lib.virginia.edu/etcbin/toccer-new2?id=TocDem1.sgm&images=images/modeng&data=/texts/english/modeng/parsed&tag=public&part=14&division=div1.

lxii.   See B. A. Robinson, "Christian Urban Legends: Did 'Einstein' prove that God exists?" *Ontario Consultants on Religious Tolerance*, latest update April 6, 2007, last accessed December 10, 2010, http://www.religioustolerance.org/culeins.htm (which offers both an account of the story and a discussion of its authenticity).

lxiii.   See Joshua 10:13.

lxiv.   See Mariana van Zeller, "Missionaries of Hate: Vanguard Trailer," *Vanguard*, June 2, 2010, last accessed December 10, 2010, http://current.com/shows/vanguard/92467622_missionaries-of-hate-vanguard-trailer.htm. This site offers the trailer to the TV report that details this legislative action and the relationship to American preachers who traveled to Uganda and encouraged the anti-gay extremism. Ugandan representatives deny that the American ministers were instrumental in creating this legislation, yet it is widely accepted that the timing of the Americans' visits is more than coincidental. This thorough report illustrates very effectively how the anti-gay measures of a section of the Christian faith engender an equally antagonistic anti-Christian sentiment. Hate is begetting hate.